THE BOKE OF KERUYNGE

THE BOKE OF KERUYNGE

(The Book of Carving)

Wynkyn de Worde

With an introduction, drawings
and glossary by
Peter Brears

SOUTHOVER PRESS
2003

This edition first published by
SOUTHOVER PRESS 2003
2 Cockshut Road, Lewes, East Sussex BN7 1JH
Copyright © Introduction, glossary, appendix
and drawings Peter Brears
A catalogue record for this book is available from the British Library
ISBN 1 870962 19 2
Typeset in Garamond 13pt by Saxon Graphics Ltd, Derby
Printed in England on wood-free paper by
Woolnough Bookbinding Ltd, Irthlingborough, Northants
for Southover Press

CONTENTS

Editor's Note

This facsimile of *The Boke of Keruynge* is published by permission of the Syndics of Cambridge University Library. I wish to thank David Hall, Deputy Librarian of the Rare Books Department, for kindly answering my questions, also Helen Hills of the same department. Christopher Whittick and Anne Brewery deciphered the interesting and angry handwriting on the Order of Precedence, and tried to identify what looks like a practice signature on the opposite page. I am grateful for their time and interest. I am indebted to Janet Clarke who, with characteristic generosity, offered to lend me F. J. Furnivall's *The Babee's Book,* (1868) which includes *The Boke of Nurture* and *The Boke of Keruynge,* both of which were useful in my interpretation of the original text. And I have to thank, as always, Nicholas and Catharine Bagnall for their unstinting work and advice.

Ann Bagnall

INTRODUCTION

IF ASKED about medieval table manners, most people at the opening of the twenty-first century will describe them in terms of raucous uninhibited gluttony, for this is how they have always seen them portrayed on film and television, and experienced them in the 'medieval banquets' staged by commercial catering establishments. The outstanding images are of Henry VIII tearing the legs off poultry before ripping at their flesh with his bare teeth – or of saucy buxom serving wenches banging down great platters heaped with coarse food. This is all pure American invention, largely stemming from Charles Laughton's famous title-role performance in *The Private Life of Henry VIII* of 1933. The truth, however, could not be in greater contrast; for the culture which produced the soaring splendours of Salisbury and Lincoln cathedrals eschewed everything crude and beastly.

Medieval society was extremely hierarchical, the boundaries between one tier and another being defined by birth, wealth, dress, and, most importantly, by manners. 'An olde proverbe Sayth... maners makyth man' wrote Alexander

Barclay in 1509, but in his day manners were far more exclusive and complex than the simple politeness and ability to eat in a restaurant which suffice in the modern world.[1] Instead of sending their young boys off to boarding school, it was customary for them to be placed as henchmen, children of honour, young gentlemen or grooms either in their own household or, more usually, those of lords of equal or preferably superior status. Here they would be trained in every aspect of courtly life, also acting as table-servants in order to be initiated into all the mysteries of its complex formality. In the Earl of Northumberland's household, for example, a henchman started looking after the cups at the end of his lord's table, there being able to observe the roles of panter, butler, waiter, cup-bearer, sewer and carver, through whose ranks he would gradually rise.[2]

It was for the benefit of these young men that the *Boke of Keruynge* was first printed in 1508 by Wynkyn de Worde. The text of at least 90% of this book was already sixty years old at this time, having been composed in the first half of the fifteenth century. Around 1430–40 an anonymous upper servant in a great medieval English household had written one of the most detailed accounts of courtly domestic service, presenting the duties of each individual officer in turn. His original manuscript now rests in the British Library, catalogued as Sloane MS 2027. The Library also houses a revision of around ten years later (Sloane MS 1351) and a final form written around 1460–70 (Harleian MS 4011). This latest version, entitled *The Boke of Nurture*, is the first to give

2

the name of its author, one John Russell, servant to that royal prince, Humphrey, Duke of Gloucester (1391–1447). As a youth, Russell had learned all the duties of panter, butler and carver, before rising to the leading posts of usher in chamber and marshal in hall in the Duke's household. Even when 'croked age' forced him into retirement, he retained a great passion for his profession, carefully recording every detail of its complex customs and practices in order to instruct youth, and so ensure its continuance into the future.[3]

Being an extremely shrewd businessman, Wynkyn de Worde clearly recognised that the *Boke of Nurture* contained a wealth of rare information which would be of great interest to his aspiring London clientele. However, a printed version of the full text would still be quite expensive and so inhibit the number of copies he could expect to sell. He therefore appears to have précised this work, transforming its original rhyming verse into prose, retaining the bulk of its practical information for serving at a lord's table, but leaving out the rules for personal table manners. Regrettably there are a number of over-simplifications, omissions and changes in punctuation in the resulting *Boke of Keruynge* which make some passages misleading, confusing, and occasionally totally mystifying, unless one returns to the original text for guidance. On page 58, for example, the carver is instructed to provide peas and frumenty to accompany 'the tayle' of a fish, but of what kind was it? Only reference back to John Russell can show that it was really a beaver's tail, a delicacy which weighed up to four pounds and, being classified as a fish,

3

could be eaten on fish days.[4] Similarly 'hony' on page 41 is actually 'heere' [hair] in the original, while on the same page we are advised to lay nine trenchers before the sovereign, rather than the five given in Russell, and on page 48 the order of carving a capon is reversed.[5]

The identification of Wynkyn de Worde's other sources is still unclear, but they too probably dated from the mid fifteenth century. From these come the verbs used to describe the methods of carving used for each individual creature, instructions for carving birds, noting their good and bad parts, and a series of seasonal menus from Easter to the feast of St John the Baptist (June 24th), at Michaelmas (September 29th), and finally on to Christmas. Further changes are made to the list of wines too, 'torrentine of Ebrew' and 'Greke' being omitted, and red wine, white wine, campolet, Rhenish, bastard and claret added in their place.

Having discussed the origins of the *Boke of Keruynge*, we may now proceed to consider the practical information it provides for the serving of medieval meals, but this is not so staightforward as might first appear. The major problem is that it was written by an expert, one who was so completely familiar with his subject that he frequently recorded all the finer points of detail, but entirely neglected to mention any of the essential basic manoeuvres which, to him, were so obvious as to be quite unnecessary to mention. We are told that the carver must not grasp a joint of venison when carving it, for example, but are not told that he must hold it down with another knife held in his left hand, in order to stop it sliding off the dish and across the pristine tablecloth.[6] We can only obtain that important detail from another contemporary source, the reading of a variety of texts, coupled with practical experimentation using real napery, tableware, cutlery and food, being absolutely essential if the true meaning of the printed instructions is ever to be thoroughly understood. A further source of confusion is provided by the lack of order in which some of the instructions are presented. These do not follow a logical progression through the meal, for the final handwashing is described well before serving and carving, for example, while sections on the carving of birds appear in the midst of the seasonal menus. These present minor problems, however, and so we can now proceed to study the practical aspects of serving a noble medieval meal as in the mid fifteenth and early sixteenth centuries.

By the mid fifteenth century noble lords had long abandoned the high table in the great hall, and now took their meals in separate chambers within their private suites. Since the routine of the Earl of Northumberland at Leconfield Castle was fully recorded in 1512, shortly after *The Boke of Keruynge* was published, we can now trace the initial arrangements for seating and serving.[7] At 10am the Earl's party washed their hands and entered the Lord's Chamber, ready for dinner, the main meal of the day. The Earl occupied the centre of one side of the table, with his countess to his left (the 'second mess') and his eldest son to his right ('the reward'). Here they were served by the Earl's second and third sons acting as carver and sewer (server) respectively, with a further gentleman to attend the eldest son. A table to one side of the chamber served as a cupboard, from which three yeomen/grooms dispensed bread, beer and wine, and two henchmen carried cups to the Earl and Countess. Another yeoman/groom at a (separate?) ewery table dispensed table cloths, napkins, towels, and the water, ewers and basins used for hand-washing. In addition, a yeoman usher supervised the chamber door, allowing access to the long procession of gentlemen waiters. Thus ten servants plus a number of waiters were required to serve just three nobles. This clearly indicates the degree of pomp and ceremony expected in a great household. After the Earl's party had dined and retired into their Drawing Chamber the food remaining on the table, supplemented by more bread and drink, provided dinner for their table servants. This whole process was then repeated for supper, served at 4pm, the servants reassembling at 7pm and then serving the Earl's livery of bread, wine etc. into his chamber at 9pm to complete their long day.

Most medieval dining tables appear to have had simple boarded tops measuring under a yard in width and supported on collapsible trestles.[8] This form of construction enabled them to be rapidly erected when required, and then dismantled and cleared away at the end of the meal. Once set up, the table was wiped clean with a cloth. Three clean tablecloths were then brought in from either the chest or the perch (hanging rail) where they had been stored. They were of pure white linen woven either in diamond-pattern 'diaper' or more ornate designs in damask, each measuring between 54 and 63 inches (137cm and 160cm) in width, and of sufficient length to almost reach the floor at both ends of the table, the third cloth perhaps being two feet (61cm) longer.[9] Each cloth had been folded down its centre line, this fold being known as 'the bought'. The first cloth or 'couch' was opened out and laid down the centre of the table, this being covered with the second cloth, its fold running along the outer edge of the table, and then the third with its fold along the inner edge. In this way the wooden table was completely covered almost to floor level, as shown in the frontispiece woodcut. To complete this process, the 'estates' had to be laid, these being six-inch (15cm) pleats folded in the third cloth at each side of the lord's place. These were easily made by placing a hand flat on the table where the estate was to be, inserting a rod beneath the cloth six inches towards the end of the table, then raising the cloth and laying it over the hand, the same then being done on the other side. The estates had the advantage of creating space for the lord's knees, which would otherwise have been pressed against a long, tight length of tablecloth.

The cup-board and ewery tables were then covered with diaper cloths, ready to receive their respective groups of utensils.[10] To the cup-board the butler brought drinking cups and clean pots full of wine and ale, and the panter brought the bread. This came in two main forms, trencher bread and manchet loaves. The first, of four day old coarse sourdough wholewheat, were not intended to be eaten, but to be sliced to provide a supply of personal cutting-boards set before each diner in the manner of modern plates. Taking a specially-designed pantry knife, the panter trimmed the trencher bread into neat sections about four inches (10cm) square, then using another sharp knife to cut them into slices, and give them smooth surfaces. In contrast, manchet loaves were individual yeast-raised white dinner buns some four inches (10cm) in diameter. Their sides had been cut all round before their second rising in order to make them tall in proportion to their width. For the lord's use, the panter chipped them with his 'chyppere' or chipping knife while still hot from the oven, trimming off four vertical slices from their sides to give them all an identical square plan. A towel of 'Reynes', alternatively called a 'portpain', being a piece of fine linen or lawn made at Rennes in Brittany measuring some ninety inches by twenty-seven (229cm×69cm) was laid flat on the cup-board, folded end to end, and a large handful of the folded end twisted tightly, just like the end of a modern toffee-paper.[11] Having secured the twisted end beneath the weight of a couple of folded towels, the long upper end of the portpain was lifted up, so that six to eight chipped manchet loaves could be laid on their sides, bottom-to-bottom in line along the centre of the lower end.[12] The upper end was then laid over the loaves, and both loose ends twisted together tightly, thus forming a neat rectangular parcel or wrapper.

Meanwhile at the ewery table basins, ewers and supplies of hot and cold water were being set out, along with a number of napkins, 'surnapes' and towels. The napkins appear to have been of linen damask, about the same size as Victorian huckaback towels, some forty-two by twenty-four inches (107cm×61cm). Folded lengthwise into four, they were placed either over the left forearm or over the left shoulder, convenient for drying the lips before or after drinking. The surnape and towels were used for the ceremonial hand-washing at the end of the meal, but had to be carefully prepared beforehand. The surnape was a long linen tablecloth probably twenty-seven inches (69cm) wide and at least a yard (92cm) longer than the table on which it was to be used, the linen towels being the same in width, but double the length. Having folded the towel end-to-end, it was placed on the surnape, and the three layers of linen folded in zig-zag pleats just under a foot (30cm) wide until they formed a neat rectangular stack, the towel's middle fold appearing at the very top. Thus prepared, it was left on the ewery table, ready for use.

Further towels measuring some 9ft 9in by 4½in (297cm×11cm) were provided for the various officers of the table, for whom they served both practical purposes and as badges of rank.[13] The carver, for example, hung his over his left shoulder and knotted it at his right hip, just like a deacon of the church or a sergeant major, while the sewer wore his in the reverse direction. The butler wore his round his neck like a priest's stole, while the waiters appear to have hung theirs over their left shoulders.

Standing at the ewery table, the butler was now 'armed' with his towel, the left end lying flat along his half-extended left arm. At the cup-board, he then hung his lord's folded napkin over his left forearm, topping this with the previously wrapped manchet loaves and three or four trimmed trencher loaves. Having picked up the principal salt with his left hand, gripping it between the folded end of his towel, he then similarly grasped both the lord's spoon and knife and the carver's knives in his right hand, and approached the table, bowing here before setting the table as shown in fig.1c, and finally covering the setting with a fine linen damask or silk cloth measuring some forty-five by twenty-seven inches (114cm×69cm) called a coverpane.[14] Once the butler had returned to the cup-board, the lord's party was ushered in from the adjoining chamber and, after grace, took their seats.

Approaching the table once more, with a bow, the butler removed the coverpane, opened one end of the portpain and placed the loaves on the table by the salt, set the lord's knife, spoon and napkin in place, put four loaves by the trenchers at each end of the table, and set a spoon and napkin for each of the other diners before kneeling and returning to the cup-board. The carver next approached the table with a bow, took up a pile of trenchers in his left hand, slipped the top of his carving knife under each in turn, and set them before the lord. The number of trenchers was dependent on the status of the lord. If of great estate, the king or a prince, he had at least five, a lower layer set four-square with another placed centrally on top. Archbishops and probably dukes had four, lords three, knights two (judging from the manuscript illustration of Sir

John Luttrell at table) and the servants in the hall just one.[15] The carver then took up one or two loaves in turn within a napkin in his left hand and dealt with them according to the personal preference of his particular lord 'wheder it be cutte in the myddes or pared or elles for to be cut in small pieces'. Apparently Duke Humphrey had one or two of his loaves pared around their edges, their upper crusts quartered and set as if whole again by the side of his knife, and the parings and lower crusts discarded. It was this practice which gave rise to the term 'upper crust' for the aristocracy.[16]

By the time the lord had taken his place at the table, the cook had set out all the food for the first course on the 'borde of sewynge' just outside the kitchen, each dish being carefully arranged in the order in which it was to be served. *The Boke of Keruynge* provides suggested menus for the periods Easter to Whitsuntide, Whitsuntide to St John's Day (June 24th), St John's Day to Michaelmas (September 29th) and Michaelmas to Christmas. From these, we learn that beef, mutton, pork, veal, capon, chicken and pigeon were available throughout these periods, while lamb, kid, young goose and eggs were popular from Easter to Whitsuntide, and bacon from the end of September to Whitsuntide. Wild birds came into season in late June, and venison, swan, heron and pheasant in late September, then being eaten through to Christmas or, more likely, to the start of Lent. No lenten menus are given, but at this period, and at numerous other fast days throughout the year, fish would have been eaten in quantity. This included salted salmon, porpoise, gurnard, lamprey, mussels and pike from

Easter to Whitsuntide, fresh salmon, halibut, bass, turbot, sole, mullet, lamprey, eels, trout and tench up to the end of June, and then sturgeon, whelks, bream and perch to the end of September.

Each dinner opened with potages with joints of (boiled?) meat. At its simplest, the potage could be the stock from the meat-boiling pot thickened with vegetables and oatmeal, but other potages were much more elaborate, these including:

Brewes Either small pieces of meat stewed with herbs and spices and thickened with rice flour, bread or eggs, or a rich meat stock poured over cubed bread.

Frumenty Hulled wheat boiled in milky broth and finished with saffron and egg yolks.

Gruel Oatmeal boiled with either ground almonds and saffron, or meat stock, ground pork and saffron.

Jowtes A selection of herbs boiled, chopped small and cooked in either rich broth or almond milk, sugar and salt.

Pease Peas, usually dried, boiled until tender, washed to remove the hulls, then reboiled and flavoured with salt, saffron, etc.

Wortes Vegetables such as cabbages, beets, leeks, nettles and various other herbs parboiled, pressed, chopped small with oatmeal and cooked in stock with salt. These, together with mustard and other piquant sauces served as accompaniments to joints of venison, beef, mutton, pork and bacon.

Next came the poultry; capons, pheasants, swans, geese and mallards, these being followed by bakemeats in the form of various pies and pasties.

The second course opened with richer potage such as:[18]

Charlet Boiled pork chopped up and cooked in an egg and milk custard, sometimes with saffron.

Jussell Grated bread mixed with saffron, salt, pepper or sage, and cooked with eggs and broth.

Marmony A typical recipe might include fried pine nuts and dates cooked with Greek wine, sugar, rice flour and spices.

Mortrus Ground boiled pork and hen cooked in broth and spices, thickened with either egg yolks and grated bread, or almond milk and rice flour.

These accompanied a selection of roast meats and poultry, supplemented by all manner of game in the autumn and winter months. As in the first course, bakemeats such as chewets (small pies), tarts and flans, fritters and 'pain puff', a rich filling within a 'loaf' of cream, flour, egg yolk and sugar pastry.[19] For Lent and the numerous fish days throughout the year, the *Boke* provides a similarly varied and luxurious menu on p58.

Once the food had been 'surveyed' to check its quality and quantity, the marshal of the hall, together with squires and sergeants of arms, accompanied the sewer's procession of servants and waiters through the great hall and on into the lord's chamber, where it was set out on the table in its predetermined order, ready for the attention of the carver.

At today's formal dinners meat is carved either in the kitchen or at a carving table in the dining room, large slices being handed to each diner, who then cuts them up into mouth-sized pieces using his or her individual knife and fork. In contrast, the carver at the medieval high table was principally concerned in providing a highly personal service by cutting each item of food in its own particular way into small portions, arranging these on their accompanying foods or with their respective sauces, and placing them before his lord or lady. They had merely to lift them to their lips with either fingers or spoon, their knives only being used for cutting some sliced foods into smaller morsels. The selection which dishes the carver should serve to the lord, and the manner in which they should be carved, required a great deal of skill, tact and observation on the part of the carver, for, as the *Boke* advises, 'kerve resonably of the flesshe to your lorde or lady & specyally for ladyes for they wyll soone be angry for theyr thoughtes ben soone chaunged, and some lordes wyll soone be pleased & some wyll not as they be of complexion'.[20]

To perform his duties successfully, the carver had to absorb a very extensive body of specialised knowledge, for each cooked joint, bird, fish or bakemeat which arrived on the table had to be carved in its own particular way, using its distinctive carving term, and its appropriate accompaniment, syrup, sprinkling or sauce. (See Appendix.) For noble meats such as venison, the carver used a second knife to hold the joint in place as he cut it up into neat squares, but all other foods were gripped with the thumb and two forefingers of his left hand. The carving knife was similarly held by the thumb and two forefingers of his right hand, the haft within his palm.[21] The carver had to be diligent in removing all 'fumosities'. These were the excessively salt, sour, tainted, fat or fried parts of joints etc., all sinews, hair, young feathers, crops, heads, pinions, skin (except the skin of waterfowl), the lower legs of all birds and beasts, and the outer sides of all birds' thighs which would cause flatulence or vaporous humours to rise up from the stomach and give the lord a headache.[22]

Venison, beef, mutton, bacon, beaver tail, salt porpoise, seal and trout were each cut into small squares and set on a bed of their particular potage, so that the lord could eat them with his spoon. Partridges, stockdoves, capons, chickens, salmon and conger eel had syrups poured over them just before they came to table, a typical syrup recipe grinding almonds with wine before stewing the resulting 'milk' with pine nuts, currants, saffron, clove, cinnamon and sugar. For these dishes choice parts of the meat were finely chopped ('minced') in the syrup, ready for the lord's spoon.[23] Plain-cooked meats such as venison, kid, rabbit and veal, together with a variety of poultry and fish, were given additional flavour at table by having ale, wine, verjuice or vinegar with sugar, salt or ground spices sprinkled on them just after being carved in their respective dishes.

Most meats and fishes were carved in slices or mouth-sized pieces and conveyed with the tip of the carving knife on to the lord's topmost trencher from where, using the two forefingers and thumb of his right hand, he perhaps dipped them into saucers of sauce or small piles of salt probably set on one of the lower trenchers, and conveyed them directly to his lips. Certain fish were served rather differently, however, baked herring being placed directly on to the lord's trencher, white herrings boned, the roes removed, and served in their dish, and the jolls (head end of the body) of salt sturgeon cut into thin morsels and arranged around the rim of the dish, for example.

The methods employed to carve each particular joint are described in great detail (see fig. 4). It should be noted that the term 'wing' in the instructions does not mean the wing alone, but actually means the wing with a substantial portion of the adjoining breast. This is stressed both by instructions to cut the wings of some birds 'large and round' and also by common sense. The lord would certainly not be satisfied with the probably overcooked meat cut from the wing-bones when the best part of the bird lay just around it. The carver called the actual wings 'pinions', and was careful to remove these as fumosities from the 'wing' portion of the breast before serving it.

Venison Hold with a second knife in the left hand, cut into squares with twelve strokes of the main carving knife, then cut the squares out and place on top of a bed of frumenty.

Bacon This meat, like most others, was gripped by the carver's left thumb and two forefingers while it was cut like venison on to a bed of pease potage.

Pheasant, partridge, stockdove & chicken Gripped by the pinion while the wing was cut off, cut into small pieces, and seasoned with either syrup or salt.

Goose, mallard, teal or swan Legs removed, then the wings, these pieces being arranged as shown, cut into six portions and served.

Peacock The wings removed and carved, the feet to be left on the legs.

Capon and large hen Wings removed, then the legs, and their flesh minced into ale or wine.

Rabbit While held on its back the skin was removed, the pelvis broken between the legs and the area around the vent cut away. A cut was then made down each side of the spine from the lower ribs down to the vent. Having been turned over on to its front, cuts were made down the side of the lower ribs, thus separating both sides from the carcase. Having been reassembled as if whole, the meat from the nape of the neck was removed, and one of the sides served to the lord.

Plaice The skin and fins removed, and the flesh cut into neat squares.

Cod, haddock, white herring and most freshwater white fish Split down the back and the skin, bones and roes removed.

Salmon, turbot, halibut, sole, carp, bream and trout The skin removed, the flesh being carved into mouth-sized pieces and placed on the lord's trencher.

Crab The meat picked from the shell, the sinews etc. removed, the meat mixed with vinegar, cinnamon and ginger, replaced in the shell and re-heated before serving.

Shrimps Removed from their shells etc. and arranged around the rim of a saucer of vinegar.

Hot pies The lid removed and the contents carved out. If the pie contained a capon, chicken or teal, it was to be lifted out on to a separate dish, the breast cut off, thinly sliced and stirred into the gravy within the pie using the point of the knife, so that the lord could eat it with his spoon.

Cold pies The top half of the crust cut away and all the contents carved.

Custards The walls cut away so that the filling and base could be cut into one inch (2.5cm) squares.

Dowcettes (small individual flans) The walls cut away to leave the lower crust intact ready for serving.

As the lord proceeded from one food to another, his topmost trencher would be removed and replaced with a fresh one to keep the various flavours quite separate. For the same reason, the carver frequently wiped his knife on his napkin throughout the meal.[24]

The final dishes served by the carver tended to be sweet. Those listed on page 38 include various bakemeats, white leach, amber jelly, cream of almonds, perch in jelly, petty peruys (small marchpanes), baked quinces, 'leche dewgarde', sage fritters, white apples or pippins with caraway comfits and wafers served with a spiced wine called hippocras. For fish days (page 58) there were to be figs, raisins, dates topped with minced ginger, roast apples and pears with sugar candy, wafers and hippocras. Further selections listed on page 28 have pears, nuts, strawberries, bilberries, white apples or pippins with caraway comfits and hard cheese recommended for the end of dinner, and roast apples and pears with a mixture of ground ginger and sugar, and hard cheese, to terminate supper. These foods were chosen for their medicinal virtues, for the sugar, spices and spiced wine were believed to warm the stomach and so aid digestion, while the hard cheese would 'kepe the stomake open'.[25] The provision of all these fresh fruits, dried fruits and sweetmeats and the preparation of the spiced wine were all the particular responsibility of the butler.

To spice the wine he ground ginger, cinnamon, grains of paradise, long pepper and turnsole and stored them seperately in bladders. A gallon of red wine was then poured into a basin, quantities of the spices stirred in with sugar, this mixture then being allowed to stand, probably at least overnight, to allow the wine to absorb the flavours. A row of six hoop-topped conical bags made of bolting cloth (probably a very fine, strong linen at this date) were then hung from a pole, their shape resembling the sleeves of the ancient Greek physician Hippocrates, hence the attributive name of hippocras for this spiced wine. After a few pints had passed through the first and second bags into the bowls set beneath, its taste was modified by adding more spices or sugar until no particular flavour predominated. The wine was then passed though the next four bags to emerge perfectly clear and ready for use.

INTRODUCTION

Now that the service of food had ended, the table was cleared, all left-overs being placed in a dish called a voider and the crumbs scooped up by the carver using his knife, probably in conjunction with a napkin. The butler then cleared away all the remaining tableware, leaving it ready for the final handwashing.

At this stage, the lord and others dining at the table all stood up while the sewer carried the previously folded towel and surnape on his shoulder from the ewery table to the left end of the dining table (see fig. 5). Here he set it down and held forward the folded end of the towel with one end of the surnape just beneath it. Now the marshal approached the table with his wooden staff twenty-seven inches long by barely half an inch in diameter (68.5cm×12cm) with one pointed end. Inserting this in the fold of the towel and gripping the end of the surnape beneath it with his thumbs, he proceeded to draw them both out along the full length of the table, bowing to the lord as he passed the centre. Kneeling at the right end of the table, he stretched the cloths straight, while the kneeling sewer held his end securely. Returning to the centre of the table, the marshal bowed to the lord, took a pace to the left, used his staff to lay a nine-inch (23cm) estate in the towel there, bowed before the lord once more, laid a further estate a pace to his right, then returned to kneel at the right end of the table, and carefully straighten the cloths there.

Now the towel and surnape were in place, the ewer of warm or cold water, perhaps scented with rosewater, together with its basin, were placed on the centre of the table where they remained until grace had been said. Two of the senior table-servants then raised each end of the estates so that the inner edge of the towel held the lord's sleeves back from his extended hands. This prevented the expensive fur or fabric of his sleeves and cuffs from being damaged by the water. The water was now poured over the lord's hands into the basin beneath, after which he dried his hands on the towel. The ewer and basin having been carried back to the ewery table, the kneeling staff stood up, the sewer using his hands, and the marshal his staff, pulled the ends of the towel and surnape straight to remove the estates, and then carried them to the centre of the table, from where the sewer returned them to the ewery table.[26]

The Boke of Keruynge gives no further details beyond this point, but from other sources we know that each of the three tablecloths were next folded up neatly, placed in the centre of the table, and handed to the panter or butler for return to the ewery table. Now that the wooden dining table stood bare once more, its top and trestles were carried away too, leaving the lord and other diners free to depart to their inner chambers.

The service of this dinner was now over, but the same ceremonial would be repeated around 4pm for supper, this regular sequence continuing every day in every great medieval English household throughout the late medieval period.

Peter Brears

21

NOTES

1   A. Barclay, *Shyp of Folys* (1509) 118

2   T. Percy (ed.), *The Earl of Northumberland's Household Book, 1512* (1903 edn) 288. Children of Honour were abolished in the royal household in 1565.

3   F. J. Furnival, *Early English Meals & Manners* (1868) pp.1–146 includes the complete text of John Russell's *Boke of Nurture.* It had first been printed for the Roxburgh Club in 1867.

4   For comparison, the following references first give the page number in the 1508 edition of *The Boke of Keruynge*, and, after the oblique stroke, the corresponding page number in Furnival's edition of Russell: Butler & Panter 1–3/4–9; Wine 3/9; Ipocras: 3–9/9; Laying the cloth 4/13; Towel 5–6/16; Setting the table 5–6/16–17; Ewery table 5/16; Sewing flesh 6–7/46–7; Serving flesh 7/48; Carving 7–8/21–22; Fumosities 8/23; Serving 8/24–5; Bakemeats 10/30; Fried meats 10/33; Potages 10/34–5; Sauces 10/35–6; Sewing fish 17/50–52; Carving fish 17–19/37–45; Sauces for fish 19/56–9; Chamberlain 19–21/59–64; Marshal, usher & precedence 21–3/70–75

5   cf. de Worde & Furnival, *op. cit.*, 8/24 line 363; 8/22 line 337 & 9/26 line 409

6   Furnival, *op. cit.,* 25 line 158

7   Percy, *op. cit.,* 287–310; 349–51

8   D. Knell, 'Tudor Furniture from the Mary Rose', *Furniture History* XI (1997) 70–72, figs.10, 11 & 15

9   D. Starkey, *The Inventory of King Henry VIII* (1998) nos. 1149–58 & W. de Worde, *Boke of Keruynge* (1508) 4

10 Percy, *op. cit.,* 359 & de Worde, *op. cit.,* 5

11 de Worde, *op. cit.,* 5 & Starkey, *op. cit.,* 11474 & 11498–9

12 de Worde, *op. cit.,* 6 or 7 loaves, Furnival, *op. cit.,* 14

13 Starkey, *op. cit.,* sewer's towels 11502–4, 17215–7; cf. R.Warner, *Antiquitates Culinariae* (1791) 100

14 Starkey, *op. cit.,* 10409–11; 11505–20; 11601; 11620; 12831; 13642; 15796; 16567; 17218–33; 17601 & 17620

15 For the numbers of trenchers see Furnival, *op. cit.,* 22; 160; 201; 352; Warner, *op. cit.,* 101 & de Worde, *op. cit.,* 8

16 de Worde, *op. cit.,* 8 & Furnival, *op. cit.,* 352

17 For references to recipes for these potage recipes see C. B. Hieatt & S. Butler, *Curye on Inglysch* (Oxford 1985) 68, 76, 87, 108; 62, 98; 98, 51; 53, 99; 62, 114. For wortes, see C. B. Hieatt, *An Ordinance of Pottage* (1988) 35

18 *Ibid.,* 107, 66, 107, 45, 68, 88, 102, 144

19 Hieatt & Butler, *op. cit.,* 204

20 de Worde, *op. cit.,* 16

21 *Ibid.,* 8

22 *Ibid.*, 8 & Furnival, *op. cit.,* 23

23 *Ibid.,* 9; Furnival, *op. cit.,* 25 line 397 & 51 line 733; & Society of Antiquaries, *Household Ordinances* (1790) 440

24 *Ibid.,* 8, Furnival, *op. cit.,* 201 line 727 advises the use of the towel.

25 *Ibid.,* 8. Both John Russell's *Boke of Nurture* and the instructions *To Serve a Lord* (Furnival, *op. cit.,* 353) suggest that the fruits, spices and sweetmeats were served at the same time as the hippocras and wafers, but other contemporary descriptions, such as that for the enthronement of Archbishop Warner in 1504 (*Household Ordinances* 114–115) have the hippocras and wafers before the handwashing and various sweetmeats with more hippocras afterwards.

26 For details of handwashing see de Worde, *op. cit.,* 5–6, Furnival, *op. cit.,* 16–17, 92–3, 351–2 & 355, and Warner, *op. cit.,* 105

Here begynneth the boke of keruynge.

HERE BEGINS the book of carving and sewing, and all the feasts in the year for the service of a prince, or any other rank. You will find the duties of each service in this book.

❦*Proper terms of a carver*

break a deer
slice brawn
rear a goose
lift a swan
sauce a capon
spoil a hen
fruche a chicken
unbrace a mallard
unlace a coney
dismember a heron
display a crane
disfigure a peacock
unjoint a bittern
untache a curlew
allay a pheasant
wing a partridge
wing a quail
mince a plover
thigh a pigeon
border a pasty
thigh a woodcock
thigh all kinds of small birds

timber a fire
tyre an egg
chine a salmon
string a lamprey
splat a pike
sauce a plaice
sauce a tench
splay a bream
side a haddock
tusk a barbel
culpon a trout
fin a chub
transon an eel
tranche a sturgeon
undertranche a porpoise
tame a crab
barb a lobster

❦**Here end the proper terms.**

❦**Here begins the butler and panter.**

You shall be butler and panter all the first year. You must have three pantry knives, one knife to square trencher loaves, another to be a chipper and the third should be

26

CHere begynneth the boke of keruynge and sewyn¬
ge / and all the feestes in the yere for the seruyce of a
prynce or ony other estate as ye shall fynde eche offyce
the seruyce accordynge in this boke folowynge

CTermes of a keruer.

Breke that dere
Lesche þ brawne
rere that goose
lyfte that swanne
sauce that capon
spoyle that henne
fruche that chekyn
vnbrace that malarde
vnlace that conye
dysmembre that heron
dysplaye that crane
dysfygure that pecocke
vnioynt that bytture
vntache that curlewe
alaye that fesande
wynge that partryche
wynge that quayle
mynce that plouer
thye that pygyon
border that pasty
thye that woodcocke
thye all maner small byrdes
tymbre that fyre

tyere that egge
chynne that samon
strynge that lampraye
splatte that pyke
sauce that place
sauce that tenche
splaye that breme
syde that haddocke
tuske that berbell
culpon that troute
fynne that cheuen
trassene that ele
traunche that sturgyon
vndertraunche that purpos
tayme that crabbe
barbe that lopster

CHere endeth the
goodly termes.

CHere begynneth
Butteler and
Panter.

THou shalte be butteler and panter all the fyrst
yere / and ye muste haue thre pantry knyues /
one knyfe to square trenchoure loues / an other to be a

27

sharp to make smooth trenchers. Chip your lord's bread hot, other bread a day old, household bread three days old and trencher bread four days old. See that your salt is white and dry, and that the ivory salt plane is two inches broad and three inches long, and that your salt cellar lid does not touch the salt. See that your table cloths, towels and napkins are neatly folded in a chest or hung upon a rail, and that your table knives are well polished and your spoons clean.

Then see that you have two augers, one larger and one smaller, bung taps made of boxwood the appropriate size, a sharp gimlet and pegs. When you set a tap on a cask make it the width of four fingers from the bottom end, slanting upwards, so that the lees do not rise. Also see that you always have butter, cheese, apples, pears, nuts, plums, grapes, dates, figs and raisins, preserved green ginger and quince marmalade. Serve on fast days: butter, plums, damsons, cherries and grapes. After meat: pears, nuts, strawberries, whortleberries and hard cheese; also white apples or pippins with caraway in comfits. After supper: roast apples and pears with blanch powder and hard cheese. Beware of cow cream and goat cream, strawberries, whortleberries and jouncat; these will make your lord ill unless he eats hard cheese. Hard cheese is an aperient and will keep the bowels open. Butter is always wholesome; it counters all poisons. Milk, cream and jouncat will close the stomach and so will a posset, so eat hard cheese and drink

chyppere / the thyrde shall be sharpe to make smothe
trenchours / than chyppe your soueraynes brede hote
and all other brede let it be a daye olde / housholde bre∫
de thre dayes olde/trenchour brede foure dayes olde/
than loke your salte be whyte and drye/the planer ma∫
de of Juory two inches brode and thre inches longe/
& loke that your salte seller lydde touche not the salte/
than loke your table clothes towelles and napkyns be
fayre folden in a cheste or hanged vpon a perche/than
loke your table knyues be fayre pullysshed & your spo∫
nes clene/than loke ye haue two tarryours a more and
a lesse and wyne canelles of boxe made accordynge &
sharpe gymlot & faucettes. And whan ye sette a pype
on broche do thus/set it foure fynger brede aboue the
nether chyme vpwardes aslaunte / and than shall the
lyes neuer aryse. Also loke ye haue in all seasons but∫
ter chese apples peres nottes plommes grapes dates
fygges and raysyns compost grene gynger and charde
quynce. Serue fastynge butter plommes damesons
cheryes and grapes. After mete peres nottes strawbe
ryes hurtelberyes & harde chese. Also brandrels or pe∫
pyns with carawey in comfetes. After souper roste ap
ples & peres with blaunche poudre & harde chese / be∫
ware of cowe creme and of goot strawberyes hurtelbe
ryes Jouncat for these wyll make your souerayne seke
but he ete harde chese/harde chese hath these operacy∫
ons/it wyll kepe the stomake open/butter is holsome
fyrst & last for it wyll do awaye all poysons/mylke cre∫
me & Jouncat they wyll close the mawe and so dooth a
posset/therfore ete harde chese and drynke romney mo
don/beware of grene saliettes & rawe fruytes for they
wyll make your souerayne seke / therfore set not mo∫

29

romney modon. Beware of green salads and raw fruits as they will make your lord ill. Avoid food that sets your teeth on edge; eat an almond and hard cheese, but do not eat much hard cheese without romney modon. If various drinks upset your lord with their vapours, let him eat a raw apple and the indigestion will cease. Moderation is good if used well; abstinence is praiseworthy if it is pleasing to God.

Inspect your wines with a candle every night, both red and sweet wine, and see that they do not referment or leak. Wash the cask heads every night with cold water and see that you have a chinching iron, adzes and linen cloths if necessary; if they referment you will hear them hiss. Therefore keep an empty cask with rose coloured lees and draw the refermented wine to the lees; it will help it. If your sweet wine pales draw it into a romney vessel to restore it.

❦Here follow the names of wines.

Red wine; white wine; claret wine; osey; capri; campolet; Rhenish wine; malvesy; bastard; tyerre romney; muscatel; clary; raspis; vernage; vernage wine cut; piment and Hippocras.

❦To make Hippocras.

Take ginger, pepper, grains of paradise, canell, cinnamon, sugar and tornsole. Then see that you have five or six bags for your Hippocras to strain into, and a rail to hang your strainers on. You must have six pewter basins to stand under your bags. Then see that your spice is ready and your ginger well pared, or beaten to a powder. Then see that

che by suche metes as wyll set your tethe on edge ther
fore ete an almonde & harde chese / but ete not moche
chese without romney modon. Also yf dyuers drynkes
of theyr fumosytees haue dyspleased your souerayne
let hym ete a rawe apple and the fumosytees wyl cease
mesure is a mery mene & it be well vsed/abstynence is
to be praysed whan god therwith is pleased. Also take
good hede of your wynes euery nyght with a candell
bothe reed wyne & swete wyne & loke they rebople not
nor leke not:& wasshe the pype hedes euery nyght with
colde water / & loke ye haue a chynchynge pron addes
and lynen clothes yf nede be,/& yf they rebople ye shall
knowe by the hyssynge / therfore kepe an empty pype
with the lyes of coloured rose & drawe the rebopled wy
ne to the lyes & it shal helpe it. Also yf your swete wyne
pale drawe it in to a romney vessell for lesynge.

¶ Here foloweth the names of wynes.

¶ Reed wyne/whyte wyne/claret wyne / osey/capry∫
ke/campolet/renysshe wyne maluesy/bastarde/tyerre
romney / muscadell/ clarrey/raspys/bernage/berna∫
ge wyne cut/pymente and Jpocras.

¶ For to make Jpocras

¶ Take gynger/peper/graynes/canell/synamon/su
ger and tornsole / than loke ye haue fyue or syxe bag∫
ges for your Jpocras to renne in & a perche that your
renners may hange on/than must ye haue. vi. peautre
basyns to stande vnder your bagges/than loke youre
spyce be redy / & your gynger well pared or it be beten

your stalks of cinnamon are well coloured and the sweet canell is not too mild. Cinnamon is hot and dry; grains of paradise are hot and moist; ginger, grains, long pepper and sugar are hot and moist; cinnamon, canell and red wine are hot and dry; tornsole is wholesome for red wine colouring. Now make sure of the quantity of your Hippocras. Then grind each of your powders separately and put them into bags made of pig's or sheep's bladders, and hang your straining bags so that they do not touch each other, but each basin should touch. Make the first basin a gallon and each of the others two quarts. Then put a gallon of red wine into your basin and add the powders and stir it well; put it into the first bag and let it run. Then put it into the second bag. Take a little in your hand and taste it to see if the ginger is strong, and mix it with cinnamon; and if the cinnamon is strong, mix it with sugar. See that you let it run through six strainers, and your Hippocras shall be the smoother. Then put your Hippocras into a closed vessel and keep the recipe, for it will serve for making sauces. Then serve your lord with wafers and Hippocras. Also see that your sweet pickles are clean and your ale is five days old before it is drunk. Be well ordered, clean and courteous to everyone. See that you do not give anyone flat ale, for it will break the scab.

When you lay the cloth wipe the table clean with a rag, then lay an under cloth called a couch. Let someone take one end of the second cloth and yourself the other end, and draw the cloth straight with the pleat on the outer edge; take the outer part and hang it even. Then take the third

to poudre / than loke your stalkes of synamon be well
coloured & swete canell is not soo gentyll in operacyon
synamon is hote and drye/graynes of paradico ben ho
te and moyste/gynger/graynes/longe peper and su/
ger ben hote and moyst/synamon/canell & reed wyne
ben hote and drye/tornsole is holsome/for reed wyne
colourynge. Now knowe ye the proporcyons of your
Ipocras / than bete your pouders eche by them selfe &
put theym in bladders & hange your bagges sure that
no bagge touche other/but let eche basyn touche other
let the fyrst basyn be of a galon and eche of the other
of a potell/than put in your basyn a galon of reed wy/
ne put therto your pouders and styre them well / than
put them in to the fyrste bagge and let it renne / than
put them in to the seconde bagge / than take a pece in
your honde and assaye yf it be stronge of gynger / and
alaye it with synamon/and it be stronge of synamon/
alaye it with suger/and loke ye lette it renne thrughe
syxe renners /& your Ipocras shall be the fyner / than
put your Ipocras in to a close bessell and kepe the re/
cepte/for it wyll serue for sewes/than serue your soue/
rayne with wafers and Ipocras. Also loke your com/
poste be fayre and clene/and pour ale fyue dayes olde
or men drynke it/than kepe your hous of offyce clene &
be curtoys of answere to eche persone/and loke ye gy/
ue no persone noo powled drynke/for it wyll breke the
scabbe. And whan ye laye the clothe wype the borde cle
ne with a cloute/than laye a cloth a couche it is called/
take your felowe that one ende & holde you that other
ende/than drawe the cloth strayght the bought on the
vtter edge/take the vtter parte & hange it euen / than
take the thyrde cloth and laye the bought on the Inner

A.iii.

cloth and lay the pleat on the inner edge, and lay an estate with the upper part of the pleat six inches wide. Then cover both your cupboard and ewery with diaper towels. Put your towel round your neck and lay one side of it upon your left arm, and place your lord's napkin on it. Place seven loaves of bread with three or four trencher loaves on your arm with the end of the towel in your left hand, in the usual way. Then take the salt cellar in your left hand and the end of the towel in your right hand to carry in the spoons and knives. Place the salt on the right side of your lord's seat, and the trenchers to the left of the salt. Then lay the knives and arrange the loaves of bread side by side, with the spoons and napkins neatly folded beside the bread. Cover your bread and trenchers, spoons and knives, and set a salt cellar with two trencher loaves at each end of the table. If you wrap your lord's bread properly you must square your bread so that all the loaves are the same size. Then make your wrapper neatly: take a Rennes towel two and a half yards long, and take the towel by the folded ends and lay it on the table. Then take a handful of the folded end and twist it hard and lay the twisted end between two towels; lay six or seven loaves bottom to bottom next to the twisted end. Then make your wrapper into a neat shape. When your lord's table is laid in this way, cover all the other tables with salt, trenchers and cups. See that your ewery is supplied with basins and ewers, and hot and cold water, and see that you have napkins, cups and spoons, and that your wine and

edge / and laye estat with the vpper parte halfe a foot
brode / than couer thy cupborde and thyne ewery with
the towell of dyaper / than take thy towell aboute thy
necke and laye that one syde of the towell vpon thy lef
te arme / and there on laye your soueraynes napkyn /
and laye on thyne arme seuen loues of brede with thre
or foure trenchour loues with the ende of the towell in
the lefte honde as the maner is / than take thy salte seller in thy lefte honde and take the ende of the towell in
your ryght honde to bere in spones and knyues / than
set your salte on the ryght syde where your souerayne
shall sytte and on the lefte syde the salte set your trenchours / than laye your knyues and set your brede one
lofe by an other / your spones and your napkyns fayre
folden besyde your brede / than couer your brede and
trenchoures spones and knyues / and at euery ende of
the table set a salte seller with two trenchour loues / &
yf ye wyll wrappe youre soueraynes brede stately ye
muste square and proporcyon youre brede and se that
no lofe be more than an other / and than shall ye make
your wrapper manly / than take a towell of reynes of
two yerdes and a halfe and take the towell by the endes double and laye it on the table / than take the ende
of the bought a handfull in your honde and wrappe it
harde and laye the ende soo wrapped bytwene two towelles vpon that ende so wrapped laye your brede botom to botom syxe or seuen loues / than set youre brede
manerly in fourme / and whan your soueraynes table
is thus arayed couer all other bordes wyth salte trenchoures & cuppes. Also se thyne ewery be arayed with
basyns & ewers & water hote and colde / and se ye haue
napkyns cuppes & spones / & se your pottes for wyne

35

ale pots are clean. Then lay the surnape reverently under a clean linen towel. Take the ends of the towel next you and the outer end of the cloth on the outer side of the table and hold these three ends together, and fold them together so that the pleat is not more than a foot wide, and smooth it in place. After meat wash with that that is at the right end of the table. You must guide it out and the marshal must carry it; see that the right side of each cloth is on the outside, and straighten it. Then you must raise the upper part of the towel and lay it smoothly; you must allow half a yard at each end of the towel so that the sewer may make an estate reverently. When your lord has washed pull the surnape straight, take it to the middle of the table and lift it up before your lord and carry it into the ewery again. And when your lord is seated see that your towel is round your neck, then bow to your lord. Then uncover your bread and put it by the salt and lay your napkin, knife and spoon before him. Then kneel on your knee till the portpain has been emptied of its eight loaves, and see that you set four loaves at the ends of the table for each mess. Make sure that every person has a napkin and spoon, and find out from the sewer how many dishes shall be served and put out the same number of cups. Then serve at table neatly so that you please everyone.

❧Here ends the butler and panter, yeomen of the cellar and the ewery. Here follows the sewing of meat.

and ale be made clene and to the furnape make ye cur∫
te∫y with a clothe vnder a fayre double napꝛy/than ta∫
ke the towelles ende nexte you /⁊ the vtter ende of the
cloth on the vtter ∫yde of the table and holde the∫e thꝛe
endes atones and folde them atones that a plyte pa∫∫e
not a foote bꝛode/than laye it euen there it ∫holde lye.
And after mete wa∫∫he with that that is at the ryghte
ende of the table/ye mu∫te guyde it out ⁊ the mar∫hall
mu∫te conuey it/and loke on eche clothe the ryght ∫yde
be outwarde and dꝛawe it ∫treyght/than mu∫t ye rep∫
∫e the vpper parte of the towell and laye it without on
gronynge/and at euery ende of the towell ye mu∫t con
uey halfe a yerde that the ∫ewer may make e∫tate reue∫
rently and lette it be. And whan youre ∫oucrayne hath
wa∫∫hen dꝛawe the ∫urnape euen/than bere the ∫urna∫
pe to the myddes of the boꝛde ⁊ take it vp befoꝛe youre
∫ouerayne ⁊ bere it in to the ewery agayne. And whan
your ∫ouerayne is ∫et loke your towell be aboute your
necke/than make your ∫ouerayne curte∫y/than vnco∫
uer youre bꝛede ⁊ ∫et it by the ∫alte ⁊ laye your napkyn
knyfe ⁊ ∫pone afoꝛe hym/than knele on your knee tyll
the purpayne pa∫∫e eyght loues/⁊ loke ye ∫et at the en∫
des of the table foure loues at a me∫∫e/and ∫e that eue∫
ry per∫one haue napkyn and ∫pone/and wayte well to
the ∫ewer how many dy∫∫hes be couered and ∫oo many
cuppes couer ye/than ∫erue ye foꝛth the table manerly
that euery man may ∫peke you curte∫y.

¶ Here endeth of the butteler and panter
yeman of the ∫eller and ewery. And here
foloweth ∫ewynge of fle∫∫he.

The sewer must arrange the dishes, and carry all the different potages, meats and sauces from the table. Every day he must find out from the cook how many dishes will be provided, and discuss with the panter and officers of the spicery which fruits are to be eaten on fast days. Then go to the sewing table and see that there are officers and servants ready to carry the dishes, and also if the marshal, squires and servants of arms will be there. Then serve your lord faultlessly.

❧Service

First set out mustard and brawn, potage, beef, stewed mutton, pheasant, swan, capon, pig, baked venison, custard, leach and lombard, meat fritters with a subtlety, two potages, blanche manger and jelly. For the main dish: roast venison, kid, fawn and coney, bustard, stork, crane, peacock with its tail, heron, bittern, woodcock, partridge, plover, rabbit, great birds, larks, doucettes, painpuff, white leach, amber jelly, cream of almonds, curlew, brewe, snipe, quail, sparrow, martins, perch in jelly, petty peruys, baked quinces, leach dewgarde, sage fritters, white apples or pippins with caraway in comfits, wafers and hippocras; all these are pleasing. Now this feast is over, clear the table.

❧Here ends the sewing of meat. Here begins the carving of meat.

The carver must know how to carve and how to handle a knife properly and how all kinds of birds should be carved. Your knife must be good and your hands must be clean.

The sewer muste sewe & from the borde conuey all maner of potages metes and sauces/ & euery daye comon with the coke and vnderstonde & wyte how many dysshes shall be and speke with the panter and offycers of the spycery for fruytes that shall be eten fastynge. Than goo to the borde of sewynge and se ye haue offycers redy to conuey and seruauntes for to bere your dysshes. Also yf marshall squyers and seruauntes of armes be there than serue forth your souerayne withouten blame.

¶ Seruyce.

¶ Fyrste sette ye forth mustarde and brawne potage befe motton stewed. Fesande/swanne/capon/pygge/venyson bake/custarde/leche and lombarde. Fruyter vaunte with a subtylte two potages blaunche manger and gelly. For standarde venyson roste kydde fawne and cony/bustarde storke crane pecocke with his tayle heronsewe bytture woodcocke partryche plouer rabettes grete byrdes larkes/ doucettes paynpuffe whyte leche ambre/gelly creme of almondes/curlewe brewe snytes quayle sparowe martynet perche in gelly/ pety perueys quynces bake/leche dewgarde fruyter fayge blandrelles or pepyns with carawaye in comfetes wafers and ypocras they be agreable/ Now this feest is done voyde ye the table.

¶ Here endeth the sewynge of flesshe. And begynneth the keruynge of flesshe.

The keruer muste knowe the keruynge and the fayre handlynge of a knyfe and how ye shall fesche all maner of fowle/ your knyfe must be fayre and

You must not put more than two fingers and a thumb upon your knife. Put the handle squarely in the middle of your hand; slice and chop finely with two fingers and a thumb; cut bread and clear crumbs with two fingers and a thumb. Make sure you never put more than two fingers and a thumb on fish, meat or fowl. Take your loaf in your left hand and hold your knife securely; wipe your knife upon your napkin so that you do not dirty the table cloth. Then take the trencher loaf in your left hand and with the edge of your table knife lift up your trenchers as near its point as you can; then set four trenchers before your lord side by side, and place two or four trenchers on them. Then take a loaf in your left hand and pare the sides; cut the upper crust for your lord and cut the lower crust and clear away the crumbs. Do not touch the loaf again after it is served. Then clean the table so that the sewer may serve your lord.

You must know the indigestible parts of fish, meat and fowls and all kinds of sauces appropriate for them. These are indigestible: salt, sour rancid fried fat, sinews, skins, hair, crops, young feathers, heads, pinions, bones, the outsides of the legs of animals and birds; never set them before your lord.

❦Service

Take your knife in your hand and cut the meat in the dish; lay it on your lord's trencher and see that there is mustard. Venison with frumenty is wholesome for your lord; do not touch the venison with your hand but only with your knife.

your handes mufte be clene & paffe not two fyngers &
a thombe vpon your knyfe. In the myddes of your hon
de fet the hafte fure vnlaffynge & mynfynge with two
fyngers & a thombe kerupnge of brede laye nge & boy٠
dynge of crommes with two fyngers and a thombe/
loke ye haue the cure/fet neuer on fyffhe / fleffhe/beeft
ne fowle more than two fyngers and a thombe / than
take your lofe in your lefte honde & holde your knyfe
furely enbrewe not the table clothe / but wype vpon
youre napkyn / than take the trenchoure lofe in youre
lefte honde and with the edge of your table knyfe take
vp your trenchours as nye the poynt as ye may / than
laye foure trenchoures to your fouerayne one by an o٠
ther/ and laye theron other foure trenchoures or elles
twayne than take a lofe in your lefte honde & pare the
lofe rounde aboute/than cut the ouer crufte to your fo٠
uerayne and cut the nether crufte & voyde the paryn٠
ge & touche the lofe no more after it is fo ferued / than
clenfe the table that the fewer maye ferue your foue٠
rayne. Alfo ye mufte knowe the fumofytees of fyffhe
fleffhe and foules & all maner of fauces accordynge to
theyr appetytes/thefe ben the fumofytees/falte foure
refty fatte fryed fenewes fkynnes hony croupes yon٠
ge feders heedes pynyons bones all maner of legges
of beeftes & fowles the vtter fyde for thefe ben fumo٠
fytees laye them neuer to your fouerayne.
¶ Seruyce.
¶ Take your knyfe in your honde and cut brawne in
the dyffhe as it lyeth & laye it on your foueraynes tren
chour & fe there be muftarde. Uenyfon with fourmen
ty is good for your fouerayne touche not the venyfon
with your honde but with your knyfe cut it. xii.draugh

41

Cut twelve slices with the edge of your knife and cut it into the frumenty. Do the same with pease and bacon, beef chine and mutton; slice the beef, cut the mutton, and set it before your lord. Beware of indigestible parts: salt, sinew, rancid and raw fat. In syrup: pheasant, partridge, stockdove and chickens: take them by the pinion in your left hand and with the point of your knife take off the wings; then chop it into the syrup. Beware of tough skin and sinew. Goose, teal, mallard and swan: take off the legs, then the wings; lay the body in the middle or in another platter, the wings in the middle and the legs behind; lay the meat between the legs and the wings in the platter. Capon or fat hen: take off the legs, then the wings, and pour on wine or ale, then chop the wing and give it to your lord. Pheasant, partridge, plover and lapwing: take off the wings, then the legs. Woodcock, bittern, egret, snipe, curlew and heron: to carve them: break off the pinions, neck and back, take off the legs, keeping the feet on, then take off the wings. A crane: take off the wings first and beware of the trump in its breast. Peacock, stork, bustard and shoveller: carve them as a crane and leave the feet on. Quail, sparrow, lark, martin, pigeon, swallow and thrush: the legs first, then the wings. Fawn, kid and lamb: give the kidney to your lord, then take off the shoulder and give your lord a rib. Roast venison: cut it in the dish and set it before your lord. A coney: lie it on its back, cut away the vents between the hind legs, break the pelvic bone, then remove the sides and separate them from the chine; lay the coney on its stomach between the two sides, and reassemble all on the dish. Cut one slice of meat

tes with the edge of your knyfe and cut it out in to the
fourmenty/doo in the same wyse with peson & bacon/
befe chyne and motton/pare the befe cut the motton/&
laye it to your souerayne/beware of fumosytees/salte
senewe fatte resty & rawe. In syrupe fesande partry=
che stokdoue & chekyns/in the left honde take them by
the pynyon & with the foreparte of your knyfe lyfte vp
your wynges / than mynce it in to the syrupe/beware
of skynne rawe & senewe. Goos tele malarde & swanne
repse the legges than the wynges/laye the body in the
myddes or in an other plater/the wynges in the myd=
des & the legges after/lay the brawne bytwene the leg
ges/& the wynges in the plater. Capon or henne of gre
ce lyfte the legges than the wynges & caste on wyne or
ale than mynce the wynge & gyue your souerayne. Fe=
sande partryche plouer & lapwinge repse the wynges &
after the legges. Woodcocke bytture egryt snyte cur=
lewe & heronsewe vnlace theym breke of the pynyons
necke & becke/than repse the legges & let the fete be on
styll than the wynges. A crane repse the wynges fyrst
& beware of the trumpe in his brest. Pecocke storke bu
starde & shoupllarde vnlace them as a crane & lette the
fete be on styl. Quaple sparow larke mertynet pygyon
swalowe & thrusshe the legges fyrste than the wynges
Fawne kydde and lambe laye the kydney to your soue=
rayne than lyfte vp the sholder & gyue your souerayne
a rybbe. Uenyson roste cut it in the dysshe & laye it to
your souerayne. A cony lay him on the backe cut away
the ventes bytwene the hynder legges breke the canell
bone than repse the sydes than laye þ cony in the wom
be on eche syde the chyne the two sydes departed from
the chyne thā laye the bulke chyne & sydes in the dysshe

into mouth-sized portions so that your lord may take it in the sauce. All hot meat pies: open the crust at the top, and all cold, at the side. Custard: cut it in inch squares for your lord. Doucettes: pare away the sides and the bottom; beware of indigestible parts. Meat fritters and sage fritters are good; pouch fritter is better. Apple fritters are good hot; but do not touch any cold fritters. Tansy is good; hot wortes, beef or mutton gruel are good. Jelly, mortrus, cream of almonds, blanche manger, jussell and charlet, cabbage and offal of deer are good. Beware of all other potages, juices, broths or sauces.

❦Here ends the carving of meat. Here begins sauces for all kinds of fowls.

Mustard is good with brawn, chine of beef, bacon and mutton. Verjuice is good with boiled chickens and capon; swan with chawdrons; ribs of beef with garlic, mustard, pepper, verjuice; ginger sauce with lamb, pig and fawn; mustard and sugar with pheasant, partridge and coney; sauce gameline with herons, egret, plover and crane. With whimbrel and curlew: salt, sugar and water of tame; with bustard, shoveller and bittern: sauce gameline. Woodcock, lapwing, lark, quail, martin, venison and snipe with white salt. Sparrows and thrushes with salt and cinnamon. Thus each meat has its appropriate sauce.

❦Here ends sauces for all kinds of fowls and meats.

Also ye must mynce foure lesses to one mozcell of mete
that pour souerayne may take it in the sauce. All bake
metes that ben hote open them aboue the coffyn & all
that ben colde open theym in the mydwaye. Custarde
cheke them inche square that pour souerayne may ete
therof. Doucettes pare away the sydes & the bottome
beware of fumosytees. Frupter vaunte frupter saye be
good better is frupter pouche apple frupters ben good
hote: and all colde frupters touche not. Tansey is good
hote woztes oz gruell of befe oz of motton is good. Gel
ly mortrus creme of almondes blauche manger Jussel
and charlet cabage and nombles of a dere ben good/&
all other potage and sewes beware of.

¶ Here endeth the keruynge of flesshe. And beginneth
sauces foz all maner of fowles.

Mustarde is good wyth brawne befe chyne ba=
con & motten. Uergyus is good to boyled che=
kyns and capon / swanne with chawdzons / rybbes of
befe wyth garlyke mustarde peper vergyus gynger/
sauce to lambe pygge & fawne mustarde & suger to fe=
sande partryche and conye / sauce gamelyne to heron
sewe egryt plouer & crane / to brewe curlewe salte su=
ger & water of tame/to bustarde shoupllarde & byttu=
re sauce gamelyne/woodcocke lapwynge larke quaple
mertynet benyson and snyte with whyte salte / spaso=
wes & throstelles with salte & synamon/thus with all
metes sauces shall haue the operacyons.

¶ Here endeth the sauces of all maner
of foules and metes.

❦Here begin the feasts and service from Easter to Whitsunday.

From Easter day to Pentecost, bread, trenchers and spoons will be laid in the usual way according to the numbers to be seated. Serve your lord thus: set trenchers before him; if he is of high rank set five trenchers, of a lower degree four trenchers, and of another degree three trenchers. Then cut the bread for your lord according to his rank, either in the middle or pared, or else in small pieces. Also you must know how meat should be served before your lord, particularly on Easter day, in accordance with the traditions of your native land.

First on that day you shall serve a boiled calf which has been blessed; then boiled eggs with green sauce, and set them before the noble of highest rank, who will share them out to those about him. Then serve potages such as greens, jowtes or brewes with beef, mutton or veal, and capons coloured with saffron, and bakemeats.

For the second course: jussell with mamony, roasted and glazed pigeons, with bakemeats such as tarts, chewets, flans and others as the cooks have decided. And at supper time various sauces for spitted mutton or veal, as directed by the steward. Then chickens with bacon, veal, roast pigeons or lamb, and roast kid with the head, and lamb with its offal, and pig's feet with vinegar and parsley on it; fried tansy and other baked meats. This form of service lasts until Pentecost, excepting fish days. Take care how you arrange

¶ Here begynneth the feestes and seruyce from
Eester vnto Whytsondaye

ON Eester daye & so forth to Pentecost after the
seruynge of the table there shall be set brede tren
chours and spones after the estymacyon of them that
shall syt there and thus ye shall serue your souerayne
laye trenchours before hym / yf he be a grete estate lay
fyue trenchours / & he be of a lower degre foure trenchours / & of an other degre thre trenchours / than cut
brede for your souerayne after ye knowe his condycy-
ons wheder it be cutte in the myddes or pared or elles
for to be cut in small peces. Also ye must vnderstonde
how the mete shall be serued before your souerayne &
namely on Eester daye after the gouernaunce & seruy
ce of the countre where ye were borne. Fyrste on that
daye ye shall serue a calfe soden and blessyd / and than
soden egges with grene sauce and set them before the
moost pryncypall estate / and that lorde bycause of his
hyghe estate shall departe them all aboute hym / than
serue potage as wortes Iowtes or browes with befe
motton or vele / & capons that ben coloured with saffron and bake metes. And in the seconde course Iussell
with mamony and rosted endoured / & pegyons wyth
bake metes as tartes chewettes & flawnes & other after the dyspolycyon of the kokes. And at soupertyme
dyuers sauces of motton or vele in broche after the or
dynaunce of the stewarde / and than chekyns with bacon vele rost pegyons or lambe & kydde roste with the
heed & the portenaūce on lambe and pygges fete with
vynegre & percely theron & a tansey fryed & other bake metes / ye shall vnderstande this maner of seruyce

47

these things before your lord. First see there are green sauces of sorrel or vines, which are sauces for the first course. Then you shall begin to carve the capon.

❧Here ends the feast of Easter until Pentecost.
❧Here begins carving of all kinds of fowls.

❧*To sauce a capon.*
Take up a capon and take off the right leg and the right wing and arrange it on the platter as if it were going to fly, and serve your lord. Capons or chickens are dressed alike, except that chickens are sauced with green sauce or verjuice.

❧*To lift a swan.*
Take and dress it like a goose, but it has more flesh. See that there is chawdron as sauce.

❧*To allay a pheasant.*
Take a pheasant and take off its legs and its wings like a hen; no sauce except salt.

❧*To wing a partridge.*
Take a partridge and take off its legs and its wings like a hen. Chop it, sauce it with wine, powdered ginger and salt. Then set it upon a chafing dish on coals to warm, and serve it.

❧*To wing a quail.*
Take a quail and take off its legs and its wings like a hen, with no sauce except salt.

❧*To display a crane.*
Take a crane and unfold its legs and cut off its wings by the joints. Then take off its wings and its legs and sauce it with powdered ginger, mustard, vinegar and salt.

dureth to Pentecoſt ſaue fyſſhe dayes. Alſo take hede
how ye ſhall araye theſe thynges befoze pour ſouerap⸗
ne/fyrſt ye ſhall ſe there be grene ſauces of ſozello2 of
ypnes that is holde a ſauce fo2 the fyrſt courſe/ and ye
ſhall begyn to repſe the capon.

¶Here endeth the feeſt of Eeſter tyll Pentecoſt. And
here begynneth keruynge of all maner of fowles.

<h3 style="text-align:center">¶Sauce that capon.</h3>

¶Take vp a capon & lyfte vp the ryght legge and the
ryght wynge & ſo araye hy fo2th & laye hy in the platet
as he ſholde flee & ſerue your ſoucrapne/& knowe well
that capons o2 chekyns ben arayed after one ſaue the
chekyns ſhall be ſauced with grene ſauce o2 vergyus.

<h3 style="text-align:center">¶Lyfte that ſwanne.</h3>

¶Take and dyghte hym as a gooſe but let hym haue
a largyour b2awne & loke ye haue chawd2on.

<h3 style="text-align:center">Alaye that feſande.</h3>

¶Take a feſande and repſe his legges & his wynges
as it were an henne & no ſauce but onely ſalte.

<h3 style="text-align:center">¶Wynge that partryche.</h3>

¶Take a partryche and repſe his legges and his wyn
ges as a henne/& ye mynce hym ſauce hym with wyne
poud2e of gynger & ſalte/ than ſet it vpon a chaufyng⸗
dyſſhe of coles to warme and ſerue it.

<h3 style="text-align:center">¶Wynge that quayle.</h3>

¶Take a quayle and repſe his legges and his winges
as an henne and no ſauce but ſalte.

<h3 style="text-align:center">¶Dyſplaye that crane.</h3>

¶Take a crane and vnfolde his legges and cut of his
wynges by the Joyntes/than take vp his wynges and
his legges & ſauce hym with pouders of gynger mu⸗
ſtarde vynegre and ſalte.

B.i.

49

To dismember a heron.

Take a heron and take off its legs and its wings like a crane, and sauce it with vinegar, mustard, powdered ginger and salt.

To unjoint a bittern.

Take a bittern and take off its legs and its wings like a heron, no sauce except salt.

To break an egret.

Take an egret and take off its legs and its wings like a heron: no sauce except salt.

To untache a curlew.

Take a curlew and take off its legs and its wings like a hen, no sauce except salt.

To untache a whimbrel.

Take a whimbrel and take off its legs and its wings in the same manner, with no sauce except salt. Then serve your lord.

To unlace a coney.

Take a coney and lay it on its back and cut away the vents. Then take off the wings and the sides and lay the trunk, chine and sides together. Sauce: vinegar and powdered ginger.

To break a sarcelle.

Take a sarcelle or a teal and take off its wings and its legs, no sauce except salt.

To mince a plover.

Take a plover and take off its legs and its wings like a hen, no sauce except salt.

A snipe.

Take a snipe and take off its wings, its legs and its shoulders like a plover, no sauce except salt.

¶ Dysmembre that heron.

¶ Take an heron and reyse his legges and his wyn¬
ges as a crane and sauce hym with vynegre mustarde
poudre of gynger and saite. ◇◇◇◇◇◇◇

¶ Untoynte that bytture

¶ Take a bytture & reyse his legges & his wynges as
an heron and no sauce but salte onely. ◇◇◇ ◇◇◇

¶ Brike that egryp.

¶ Take an egryp and reyse his legges and his wynges
as an heron and no sauce but salte. ◇◇◇ ◇◇◇ ◇◇◇

¶ Untache that curlewe.

¶ Take a curlewe and reyse his legges and his wyn¬
ges as an henne and no sauce but salte.

¶ Untache that brewe.

¶ Take a brewe and reyse his legges and his wynges
in the same maner and no sauce but onely salte & serue
your soueraŷne.

¶ Unlace that cony.

¶ Take a cony and laye hym on the backe & cut awaye
the bentes / than reyse the wynges and the sydes and
laye bulke chyne and the sydes togyder sauce vynegre
and poudre of gynger.

¶ Breke that farsel'.

¶ Take a farsell or a teele and reyse his wynges and
his legges and no sauce but salte onely.

¶ Mynce that plouer.

¶ Take a plouer and reyse his legges and his wynges
as an henne and no sauce but onely salte

¶ A snyte.

¶ Take a snyte and reyse his wynges his legges and
his sholders as a plouer and no sauce but salte. ◇◇◇

¶ Thye that woodcocke

Take a woodcock and take off its legs and its wings like a hen; this done, dress the brain.

Here begins the feast from Pentecost until midsummer.

In the second course from Pentecost to the feast of Saint John the Baptist for the meats already mentioned, use wine, ale, vinegar and powders, ginger and canell as sauces for the appropriate meat.

The first course should be boiled or roasted beef or mutton with capons. If the capons are boiled, dress them as before; when they are roasted throw on salt with wine or ale. Then take the capon by the legs and pour on the sauce; carve it and arrange it on a dish looking ready for flight. First you must cut the right leg and the right shoulder; and between the four limbs lay the meat of the capon with the crop between the legs to look as though all was joined together again. Other bakemeats follow after.

In the second course the potage shall be jussell, charlet or mortrus, with roasted young geese, veal, pork, pigeons or chickens, with painpuff, fritters and other bakemeats as the cook has decided. The goose ought to be cut limb to limb beginning with the right leg, and so on to under the right wing and not upon the joint above. It should be eaten with green garlic, sorrel, tender vines or verjuice in the summer, as your lord wishes. You should know that all fowls with whole feet should be carved under the wing and not above.

Here ends the feast from Pentecost to midsummer.

¶ Take a woodcocke & repse his legges and his wyn= ges as an henne this done dyght the brayne. And here begynneth the feeſt from Pentecoſt vnto mydſomer.

IN the seconde courſe for the metes before sayd ye ſhall take for your ſauces wyne ale vynegre and pouders after the mete be & gynger & canell from Pentecoſt to the feeſt of saynt Johan baptyſt. ¶ The fyrſt courſe ſhall be befe morton soden with capons or roſted/& yf the capons be soden araye hym in the ma= ner aforeſayd. And whan he is roſted thou muſt caſte on ſalte with wyne or with ale/than take the capon by the legges & caſte on the ſauce & breke hym out & laye hym in a dyſſhe as he ſholde flee. fyrſt ye ſhall cut the ryght legge & the ryghte ſholder/& bytwene the foure membres laye the brawne of the capon with the crou= pe in the ende bytwene the legges as it were poſſyble for to be Joyned agayne togyder/& other bake metes after. And in the seconde courſe potage ſhall be Juſſell charlet or mortrus with yonge geeſe bele porke pegy= ons or chekyns roſted with payne puffe/fruytets and other bake metes after the ordynaūce of the boke . Al= so the gooſe ought to be cut membre to membre begyn nynge at the ryght legge & soo forth vnder the ryghte wynge & not vpon the Joynte aboue/& it ought for to be eten with grene garlykc or with soreil or tender vy= nes or vergyus in somer seaſon after the pleaſure of your souerayne. Also ye ſhall vnderſtande that all ma ner of fowle that hathe hole fete ſholde be repſed vn= der the wynge and not aboue. ☙☙☙

¶ Here endeth the feeſt from Pentecoſt to mydſomer.

53

❦Here begins the feast of Saint John the Baptist until Michaelmas.

For the first course: potage: greens, gruel, frumenty with venison and mortrus; legs of pork with green sauce, roasted capon, and swan with chawdron.

For the second course: potage as directed by the cooks, with roasted mutton, veal, pork, chickens or glazed pigeons, herons, fritters or other bakemeats. See that the pheasant is dressed in the style of a capon, but dry without any moisture and eaten with salt and powdered ginger. The heron should be dressed in the same way without any moisture, and should be eaten with salt and powder. You should know that all kinds of fowls with open claws like a capon should be carved and dressed like a capon.

❦From the feast of Saint Michael until the feast of Christmas.

For the first course: potage: beef, mutton, bacon, legs of pork; or with goose, capon, mallard, swan or pheasant as before said; with tarts, bakemeats or chines of pork.

For the second course: potage: mortrus, conies or sewe. Then roast meat: mutton, pork, veal, pullets, chickens, pigeons, teals, widgeons, mallards, partridge, woodcock, plover, bittern, curlew, heron, venison, great birds, snipe, fieldfares, thrushes, fritters, chewettes, beef with sauce

And here begynneth from the feeſt of ſaynt Johñ the baptyſt vnto Myghelmaſſe.

IN the fyrſt courſe potage woꝛtes gruell ⁊ four menty with venyſon and moꝛtrus and peſtelles of poꝛke with grene ſauce. Roſted capon ſwanne with chawdꝛon. In the ſeconde courſe potage after the oꝛ dynaunce of the cokes wyth roſted motton vele poꝛke chekyns oꝛ endoured pygꝛons heron ſewes fruyters oꝛ other bake metes / and take hede to the feſande he ſhall be arayed in the maner of a capon / but it ſhall be done dꝛye wythout ony moyſture and he ſhall be eten with ſalte and pouder of gynger. And the heronſewe ſhall be arayed in the ſame maner without ony moyſ ſture and he ſholde be eten with ſalte and poudꝛe. Alſo ye ſhall vnderſtande that all maner of fowles hauynge open clawes as a capon ſhall be tyred and arayed as a capon and ſuche other.

¶ From the feeſt of ſaynt Myghell vnto
the feeſt of Cryſtmaſſe.

IN the fyrſt courſe potage befe motton bacon oꝛ peſtelles of poꝛke oꝛ with gooſe capon mallarde ſwanne oꝛ feſande as it is befoꝛe ſayd with tartes oꝛ bake metes oꝛ chynes of poꝛke. In the ſeconde courſe potage moꝛtrus oꝛ conyes oꝛ ſewe / than rooſt fleſſhe motton poꝛke vele pullettes chekyns pygꝛons teeles wegyons mallardes partryche woodcorke plouer byt tute curlewe heronſewe / venyſon rooſt grete byrdes ſnytes feldefayres thꝛuſſhes fruyters chewettes befe with ſauce gelopere rooſt with ſauce pegyll ⁊ other ba

gelopere, roast beef with sauce pegyll, and other bakemeats as before said. If you carve any boiled meat before your lord or your lady, carve away the skin on top. Then carve the meat carefully for your lord or lady, and specially for ladies, for they become angry and changeable quickly. Some lords are easily pleased and some are not, depending on their temperament. The goose and swan may be carved as other birds with whole feet left on, or else as your lord or lady wishes. Also a swan with chawdron, capon or pheasant, should be dressed as before said; but the skin must be taken off when they are carved before your lord or your lady; for generally the skin of cloven-footed fowls is unwholesome, and the skin of whole-footed fowls is wholesome to eat. Also you must know that all kinds of whole-footed fowls that live on water have wholesome and clean skins, for they are cleansed by the water, and live off fish. If they eat any stinking thing, the water cleanses the foulness from them. The skins of capons, hens or chickens are not so clean, for they eat foul things on the ground and their skins are not wholesome; it is not their nature to go into the river to clean their flesh. Mallard, geese and swans eat foul things on land, but then clean themselves of their foul stink in the river. A pheasant is as before said, but the skin is not wholesome. Take off the heads of all field and wood birds such as pheasant, peacock, partridge, woodcock and curlew, for they also eat foul things as worms, toads and suchlike.

❧Here ends the feasts and the carving of meat.

ke metes as it is aforesayd. And yf ye kerue afore your
lorde or youre lady ony soden flesshe kerue awaye the
skynne aboue/than kerue resonably of þ flesshe to your
lorde or lady & specyally for ladyes for they wyll soone
be angry for theyr thoughtes ben soone chaunged/and
some lordes wyll soone be pleased & some wyll not /as
they be of complexion. The goose & swanne may be cut
as ye do other fowles þ haue hole fete or elles as your
lorde or your lady wyll aske it. Also a swanne w chaw
dron capon or fesande ought for to be arayed as it is a-
fore sayd/but the skynne must be had awaye/& whan
they ben kerued before your lorde or your lady/for generally the skynne of all maner clouen foted fowles is
vnholsome / & the skynne of all maner hole foted fowles ben holsome for to be eten. Also wyte ye well that al
maner hole foted fowles that haue theyr lyuyng vpon
the water theyr skynnes ben holsome & clene for by the
clenes of the water/& fysshe is theyr lyuynge. And yf
that they ete ony stynkynge thynge it is made so clene
with the water that all the corrupcyon is clene gone a-
way from it. And the skynne of capon henne or chekyn
ben not so clene for they ete foule thynges in the strete/
& therfore theyr skynnes ben not holsome/for it is not
theyr kynde to entre in to þ ryuer to make theyr mete
voyde of the fylth. Mallarde goose or swanne they ete
vpon the londe foule mete/but anone after theyr kynde
they go in to the ryuer & there they clense them of theyr
foule stynke. A fesande as it is afore sayd/but þ skynne
is not holsome/than take the heedes of all felde byrdes
and wood byrdes as fesande pecocke partryche wood
cocke and curlewe for they ete in theyr degrees foule
thynges as wormes todes and other suche.

                                            B.iii.

                        57

❦Here begins the sewing of fish.

❦*The first course.*

The sewing of fish: mussels, minnows in porpoise or salmon stew, bacon, herring with sugar, green fish, pike, lamprey, salens, roast porpoise, baked gurnard and baked lamprey.

❦*The second course.*

White and red jelly, dates in comfits, conger, salmon, dory, brill, turbot, halibut. For the main dish: bass, trout, mullet, chub, sole, eels, roast lampreys and tench in jelly.

❦*The third course.*

Fresh sturgeon, bream, perch in jelly, head of salmon, sturgeon, whelks, and apples and pears roasted with sugar candy. Figs of Malyke, raisins, dates stuffed with chopped ginger, wafers and Hippocras are agreeable. This feast is done. Clear the table.

❦Here ends the sewing of fish. Here follows the carving of fish.

The fish carver must see that the tail and the liver are put into the pease broth and frumenty. If there is salt porpoise, seal or tuna, prepare it the same way as venison. Baked herring: lay it whole upon your lord's trencher. White herring in a dish: open it by the back, pick out the bones and the roe, and see there is mustard. Salt fish, green fish, salt salmon and conger: pare away the skin. Salt fish, stock fish, marlin, mackerel, and hake with butter: take away the bones and the skins. Pike: lay it stomach down on the

¶Here endeth the feestes and the keruynge of flesshe. And here begynneth the sewynge of fysshe.

¶The fyrst course.

TO goo to sewynge of fysshe musculade menes wes in sewe of porpas or of samon bacon he/tynge wyth suger grene fysshe pyke lampraye salens porpas rosted bake gurnarde and lampraye bake

¶The seconde course.

¶Gelly whyte and reed dates in comfetes congre salmon dorrey bytte turbot halybut / for standarde base troute molette cheuene sole eles and lamprayes roost tenche in gelly.

¶The thyrde course.

¶Fresshe sturgyon breme perche in gelly a Joll of samon sturgyon and welkes apples & peres rosted with suger candy. Fygges of malyke & taylyns dates capte with mynced gynger / wafers and Ipocras they ben agreable/this feest is done voyde ye the table.

¶Here endeth sewynge of fysshe. And here foloweth keruynge of fysshe.

THe keruer of fysshe must se to pessene and four/mentye the tayle and the lyuer ye muste loke yf there be a salts purpos or sele turrentyne & do after the fourme of venyson / baken herynge laye it hole vpon pour soueraynes trenchout/whyte herynge in a dysshe open it by the backe pyke out the bones & the rowe & se there be mustarde. Of salte fysshe grene fysshe salte samon & congre pare away the skyn / salte fysshe stocke fysshe marlynge makrell and hake with butter take away the bones & the skynnes. A pyke laye the wombe vpon his trenchour with pyke sauce ynoughe. A salte

59

trencher with enough pike sauce. Salt lamprey: cut it into seven or eight thick slices and set it before your lord. Plaice: drain the water, then cross it with your knife, add salt, wine or ale. Gurnard, red gurnard, bream, chub, bass, mullet, roach, perch, sole, mackerel, whiting, haddock and codling: cut them down the back, take out the bones and clean the belly of entrails. Carp, bream, sole and trout: back and belly together. Salmon, conger, sturgeon, turbot, thorpole, thornback, houndfish and halibut: cut them in the dish like a porpoise. Tench in its sauce: cut it. Eels and roast lampreys: pull off the skin, take out the bones, add vinegar and powder. Crab: break it apart into a dish, clean the shell, replace the meat, season it with vinegar and powder, then cover it with breadcrumbs and send it to the kitchen to heat. Then set it before your lord and break the large claws and lay them in a dish. Crayfish: dress it thus: break it apart, slit the belly and take out the flesh, cut away the red skin and chop it thin; put vinegar in the dish and set it on the table without heat. Head of sturgeon: cut it in thin pieces and lay it round about the dish. Fresh baked lamprey: open the pasty; then take white bread, cut it thin, lay it in a dish, and with a spoon cover the bread with the galantine juices from the pasty, red wine and powdered cinnamon. Then cut a chunk of the lamprey, chop it thin and lay it in the galantine and set it upon the fire to heat. Fresh herring: with salt and wine. Shrimps: well cleaned. Flounders, gudgeons, minnows, mussels, eels, lampreys and sprats are good in stew. Mussels: with greens. Oysters: in chive sauce or in gravy. Minnows, porpoise, salmon and seal in white and red jelly; cream of almonds, dates in comfits, pears and

lampraye goboneit flatte in. bii. o2. biii. peces & laye it
to pour fouerayne. A playce put out the water / than
croffe hym with pour knyfe caft on falte & wyne o2 ale.
Go2narde rochet b2eme cheuen bafe molet roche per
che fole makrell & whptynge haddocke and coblynge
repfe theym by the backe & pyke out the bones & clenfe
the refet in the belly. Carpe b2eme fole & troute backe &
belly togyder. Samon congre fturgyon turbot tho2
pole tho2bake hounde fpffhe & halybut cut them in the
Dpffhe as the po2pas aboute / tenche in his fauce cut it
eles & lamp2ayes rooft pull of the fkynne pyke out the
bones put therto bynegre and poud2e. A crabbe b2eke
hym a fonder in to a Dpffhe make the fhelle clene & put
in the ftuffe agayne temp2e it wyth bynegre & pouder
than couer it with b2ede and fende it to the kytchyn to
hete / than fet it to pour fouerayne and b2eke the grete
clawes and laye them in a Dpffhe. A creues dpght hym
thus departe hym a fonder & flytte the belly and take
out the fpffhe pare away the reed fkynne and mynce it
thynne put bynegre in the Dpffhe and fet it on the table
without hete. A Jol of fturgyon cut it in thynne mo2fel
les & laye it rofide aboute the Dpffhe. Freffhe lamp2aye
bake open the pafty / than take whyte b2ede and cut it
thynne & laye it in a Dpffhe & with a fpone take out ga
lentyne & laye it bpon the b2ede with reed wyne & pou
der of fynamon / than cut a gobone of the lamp2aye &
mynce the gobone thynne and laye it in the galentyne
than fet it bpon the fyre to hete. Freffhe herpnge with
falte & wyne / fh2ympes well pyked flouders gogyons
menewes & mufceles eles and lamp2ayes fp2ottes is
good in fewe / mufculade in wo2tes / opfters in ceuy oy
fters in grauy menewes & po2pas famon & feele gelly

61

quinces in syrup with parsley roots, mortrus of houndfish.
Rise. Stand.

❧Here ends the carving of fish. Here begins sauces for all kinds of fish.

Mustard is good with salt herring, salt fish, salt conger, salmon, sparling, salt eel and ling. Vinegar is good with salt porpoise, salt tuna, salt sturgeon, thorpole and salt whale; galantine with lamprey; verjuice with roach, dace, bream, mullet, bass, flounders, sole, crab; powdered cinnamon with chub. With thornback, herring, houndfish, haddock, whiting and cod: vinegar, powdered cinnamon and ginger. Green sauce is good with green fish, halibut, cuttlefish and fresh turbot. Do not put your green sauce away, it is good with mustard.

❧Here ends the appropriate sauces for each kind of fish.

❧*The chamberlain*

The chamberlain must be clean and diligent in his duties, with his hair combed before carefully attending to his lord. See that he has a clean shirt, breeches, petticoat and doublet; then brush his hose, inside and out, and see that his shoes and slippers are clean. In the morning when your lord rises, warm his shirt by the fire, and see that he has a foot sheet made in this way: first set a chair by the fire with a cushion and another under his feet, then spread a sheet over the chair and see there is a neckcloth and a comb

whyte and reed creme of almondes dates in comfetes peres and quynces in syrupe wyth percely rotes mortrus of houndes fysshe ryse standynge.

¶ Here endeth the keruynge of fysshe. And here begynneth sauces for all maner of fysshe.

Mustarde is good for salte herynge salte fysshe salte congre samon sparlynge salte ele & lynge vynegre is good wyth salte porpas turrentyne salte/ sturgyon salte threpole & salte wale/lampray with galentyne/vergyus to roche dace breme molet basc flouders sole crabbe & cheuene with pouder of synamon/ to thornebacke herynge houndefysshe haddocke whytynge & codde vynegre pouder of synamon & gynger grene sauce is good with grene fysshe and halybut cottell and fresshe turbot/put not pour grene sauce away for it is good with mustarde.

¶ Here endeth for all maner of sauces for fysshe accordynge to theyr appetyte. ❧❧❧❧ *
¶ The chaumberlayne.

The chaumberlayne muste be dylygent & clenly in his offyce with his heed kembed & soo to his souerayne that he be not recheles and se that he haue a clene sherte breche petycote and doublet/than brusshe his hosen within & without and se his shone & slyppers be made clene/& at morne whan your souerayne wyll aryse warme his sherte by the fyre/& se he haue a foot shete made in this maner. Fyrst set a chayre by the fyre with a quysshen an other vnder his fete / than sprede a shete ouer the chayre & se there be redy a kerchefe

ready. Warm his petticoat, doublet and stomacher and put on his hose and his shoes or slippers. Pull up his hose neatly and tie them up. Then lace his doublet hole by hole and lay his neckcloth round him and comb his hair. See that you have a basin and ewer with warm water and a towel, and wash his hands. Then kneel upon your knee and ask your lord what robe he wishes to wear; bring him what he orders and put it on him. Then place his girdle round him and take your leave courteously. Go to the church or chapel to your lord's closet, lay carpets and cushions and put out his prayer book. Then draw the curtains and take your leave and go to your lord's chamber and take all the clothes off his bed, beat the featherbed and the bolster, but be careful not to shed feathers. Then shake the blankets and see the sheets are sweet and clean, or that you have clean sheets. Make up his bed neatly and lay the head sheets and pillows. Then take up the towel and the basin; lay carpets round the bed or windows, and lay carpets and cushions on the cupboards. See there is a good fire burning bright, and see the house of easement is sweet and clean and the privy board is covered with a green cloth and a cushion, and see that there is some white woollen cloth, down or cotton for your lord. See that you have a basin and ewer with water and a towel for your lord. Then take off his gown, and bring him a mantle to keep him from getting cold; bring him to the fire and take off his shoes and his hose. Take a fine Rennes cloth and comb his hair; put on his neckcloth

and a combe/than warme his peticote his doublet and
his ſtomachere/& than put on his hoſen & his ſhone or
ſlyppers than ſtryke vp his hoſen manerly & tye them
vp than laſe his doublet hole by hole & laye the clothe a
boute his necke & kembe his heed/than loke ye haue a
baſyn & an ewere with warme water and a towell and
waſſhe his hondes / than knele vpon your knee & aſke
your ſouerayne what robe he wyll were & brynge hym
ſuche as your ſouerayne cōmaūdeth & put it vpon hym
than doo his gyrdell aboute hym & take your leue ma⸗
nerly & go to the chyrche or chapell to your ſoueraynes
cloſet & laye carpettes & quyſſhens & lay downe his bo⸗
ke of prayers / than drawe the curtynes and take your
leue goodly & go to your ſoueraynes chambre & caſt all
the clothes of his bedde & bete the federbedde & the bol
ſter/but loke ye waaſt no feders than ſhake the blanket
tes & ſe the ſhetes be fayre & ſwete or elles loke ye haue
clene ſhetes/than make vp his bedde manerly than lay
the heed ſhete & the pyllowes/than take vp the towel &
the baſyn & laye carpettes aboute the bedde or wyndo⸗
wes & cupbordes layde with carpettes and quyſſhens:
Alſo loke there be a good fyre brennynge bryght / & ſe
the hous of eſement be ſwete & clene & the preuy borde
couered with a grene clothe & a quyſſhen/than ſe there
be blanket donne or cotton for your ſouerayne / & loke
ye haue baſyn & ewere with water & a towel for your ſo
uerayne/than take of his gowne/& brynge hym a man
tell to kepe hym fro colde/than brynge hym to the fyre
& take of his ſhone & his hoſen than take a fyne kercher
of reynes & kembe his heed & put on his kercher & his
bonet/than ſprede downe his bedde laye the heed ſhete
and the pyllowes/& whan your ſouerayne is to bedde

and nightcap. Then turn down his bed and arrange the head sheet and the pillows. When your lord goes to bed draw the curtains, and see there is a nightlight, wax or candle ready. Then drive out the dog or cat and see that there is a night-stool and urinal set near your lord. Then take your leave courteously so that your lord may take his rest merrily.

❦Here ends the chamberlain.

❦Here follow the marshal and the usher.

The marshal and the usher must know the precedence of all the ranks of the church and the estate of the king and blood royal.

❦The estate of a Pope has no equal.
❦The estate of an emperor is next.
❦The estate of a king.
❦The estate of a cardinal*.
❦The estate of a king's son, a prince.
❦The estate of an archbishop.
❦The estate of a duke.
❦The estate of a bishop.
❦The estate of a marquess.
❦The estate of an earl.
❦The estate of a viscount.
❦The estate of a baron.
❦The estate of an abbot with a mitre.
❦The estate of the three chief judges and the mayor of London.
❦The estate of an abbot without a mitre.

drawe the curtynes / than se there be morter or ware
or perthoures be redy / than dryue out dogge or catte &
loke there be basyn and vrynall set nere your soueray=
ne / than take your loue manerly that your souetayne
may take his rest meryly.

¶ Here endeth of the chaumberlayne.

¶ Here foloweth of the Marshall and the vssher.

The Marshall and the vsshere muste knowe all
the estates of the chyrche and the hyghe estate
of a kynge with the blode royall.

¶ The estate of a Pope hath no pere
¶ The estate of an Emperour is nexte
¶ The estate of a kynge
¶ The estate of a cardynall
¶ The estate of a kynges sone a prynce
¶ The estate of an archebysshop
¶ The estate of a duke
¶ The estate of a bysshop
¶ The estate of a Marques
¶ The estate of an erle
¶ The estate of a vycount
¶ The estate of a baron
¶ The estate of an abbot with a myter
¶ The estate of the thre chefe Iuges and the
mayre of London.
¶ The estate of an abbot without a myter
¶ The estate of a knyght bacheler
¶ The estate of pryour dene archedeken or knyght

67

- The estate of a knight bachelor.
- The estate of prior, dean, archdeacon or knight.
- The estate of the master of the rolls.
- The estate of other justices and barons of the chequer.
- The estate of the mayor of Calais.
- The estate of a provincial doctor divine.
- The estate of a protonotary who is above the pope's collector and a doctor of both laws.
- The estate of an ex-mayor of London and servant of the law.
- The estate of a master in chancery and other worshipful preachers of pardon, clerks in holy orders, all other orders of celibates, parsons and priests, worshipful merchants and gentlemen: these may sit at the squire's table.
- An archbishop and a duke may not dine in hall but each estate by themselves in a separate chamber, or pavilion.
- Bishops, marquesses, earls and viscounts: all these may sit two to a mess.
- A baron, the mayor of London, the three chief judges, the speaker of parliament and an abbot with a mitre: all these may sit two or three to a mess.
- All other estates may sit three or four to a mess.
- The marshal must know the royal lineage, for some lords are of royal blood and of small inheritance. A lady of royal blood keeps her rank if married to a knight. A lady of lower degree takes her husband's rank. Thus the blood royal shall be given the respect due to it.

¶ The eſtate of the mayſter of the rolles
¶ The eſtate of other Juſtyces & barons of the cheker
¶ The eſtate of the mayre of Calays
¶ The eſtate of a prouyncyall a doctour dyuyne
¶ The eſtate of a prothonat he is aboue the popes col
lectour and a doctour of bothe lawes
¶ The eſtate of hym that hath ben mayre of London
and ſeruaunt of the lawe.
¶ The eſtate of a mayſter of the chauncery and other
worſhypfull prechours of pardon and clerkes that
ben gradewable / & all other ordres of chaſtyte per
ſones and preeſtes worſhypfull marchauntes & gen
tylmen all theſe may ſyt at the ſquyers table.
¶ An archebyſſhop and a duke may not kepe the hall
but eche eſtate by them ſelfe in chaumbre or in pauy
lyon that nother ſe other.
¶ Byſſhoppes Marques Erles & Uycountes all theſe
may ſyt two a meſſe.
¶ A baron & the mayre of London & thre chefe Juges
and the ſpeker of the parlyament & an abbot with
a myter all theſe may ſyt two or thre at a meſſe
¶ And al other eſtates may ſyt thre or foure at a meſſe
¶ Alſo the Marſhall muſte vnderſtonde and knowe
the blode royall for ſome lorde is of blode royall and
of ſmall lyuelode. And ſome knyghte is wedded to
a lady of royall blode ſhe ſhal kepe the eſtate that ſhe
was before. And a lady of lower degree ſhall kepe
the eſtate of her lordes blode / and therfore the royal
blode ſhal haue the reuerence as I haue ſhewed you
here before.
¶ Alſo a Marſhall muſte take hede of the byrthe and
nexte of the lyne of the blode royall.

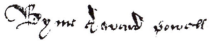

69

❧The marshal must be aware of the birth and next in line of the blood royal.

❧Also he must be aware of the king's officers: the chancellor, steward, chamberlain, treasurer and controller.

❧The marshal must welcome strangers and show them respect in honour of your lord.

❧The marshal must take note if any message is sent to your lord from the king; and if he sends a knight, receive him as a baron; if he sends a squire, receive him as a knight; if he sends a yeoman, receive him as a squire; if he sends a groom, receive him as a yeoman.

❧It is not disrespectful to a knight to seat a king's groom at his table.

Here ends the book of service, carving and sewing, and all kinds of office to a prince or any other rank, and all the feasts during the year. Printed by Wynkyn de Worde in Fleet Street, London, at the Sign of the Sun. In the Year of our Lord MCCCCCVIII.

Wynkyn de Worde

*The margin has been cropped. The handwriting reads:
    [thi]s downe [l]ower
    [t]o this place.
The effect is to move *Cardinal* between *Duke* and *Bishop.*
The pen-trial on the opposite page reads:
    By me Edward Dowell [*or perhaps* Cowell]

¶ Also he muſt take hede of the kynges offycers of the Chaunceler Stewarde Chamberlayne Treſourer and Controller.

¶ Also the Marſhall muſt take hede vnto ſtraungers & put them to worſhyp & reuerence for & they haue good chere it is your ſouerarynes honour.

¶ Also a Marſhall muſte take hede yf the kynge ſen= de to your ſouerayne ony meſſage and yf he ſende a knyght receyue hym as a baron / and yf he ſende a ſquyere receyue hym as a knyght / and yf he ſende a yeman receyue hym as a ſquyer / and yf he ſende a grome receyue hym as a yeman.

¶ Also it is noo rebuke to a knyght to ſette a grome of the kynge at his table.

¶ Here endeth the boke of ſeruyce and keruynge and ſewynge and all maner of offyce in his kynde vnto a prynce or ony other eſtate and all the feeſtes in the yere. Enprynted by Wynkyn de Worde at London in the Fleteſtrete at the ſygne of the ſonne. The ye= re of our lorde; M.CCCCC.viij.

71

DRAWINGS
AND
EXPLANATIONS

1

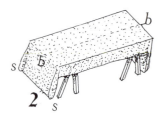

2

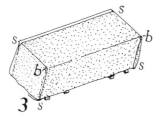

3

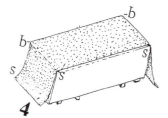

4

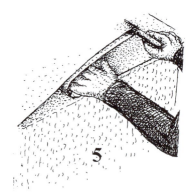

5

Figure 1

A. Laying the tablecloths

In this caption b represents the bought or central fold of each tablecloth, and s the selvedge. **1**– The table is erected. **2**– The first cloth or couch is laid centrally **3**– The second cloth is laid with its central fold along the front of the table. **4**– The third cloth is laid with its central fold along the lord's side of the table. **5**– (Using a staff), the butler folds estates six inches (15cm) wide in the third cloth, their pleats facing the ends of the table. **6**– The completed tablecloths.

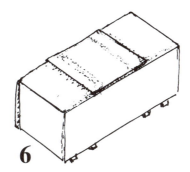

B. Wrapping the bread

1– The portpain is folded double and the folded end twisted. **2–** Holding the twist in place beneath the weight of two napkins, the top part of the portpain is then folded back over the napkins. **3–** Six pared loaves are placed bottom-to-bottom on the lower half of the portpain, which is then folded over them. The top part is then folded back over the top. **4–** The open ends of the portpain are twisted together and folded beneath to form a compact parcel. **5**

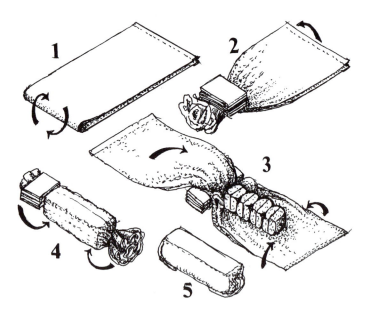

C. Arming towels

1– The carver's arming towel was worn diagonally over his left shoulder (*Pageant of the Life of the Earl of Warwick 1389–1439*). **2–** The sewer's, diagonally over his right shoulder. **3–** The waiter's, over his left shoulder, and probably tied tight beneath his armpit, leaving the two ends free to grasp dishes etc. (*Field of the Cloth of Gold*, mid 16th century). **4–** The butler's, hung round his neck and falling to the front. (W. Caxton, no. 375, late 15th century). **5–** A butler using his towel to carry the carving knives, eating knife and spoon in the right hand, and the salt, napkins, folded portpain and trencher loaves in his left, ready to lay the table.

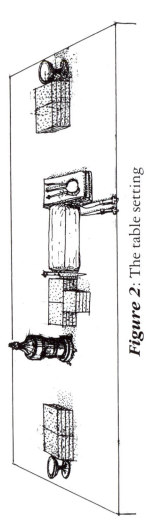

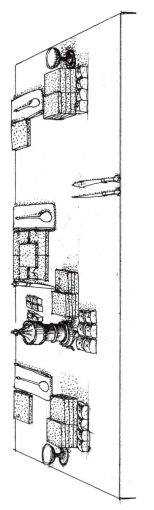

Figure 2: The table setting

Above, we see the table as laid by the butler just before being covered by its fine coverpane cloth, ready for the lord to take his place. When he was seated, the butler removed the coverpane, opened one end of the portpain and set the loaves on the table near the salt, put more loaves by the trenchers at each end of the table, and arranged cutlery and a napkin before each diner. At this point the carver approached the table, set the trenchers in place, and so completed the table setting, as seen below.

78

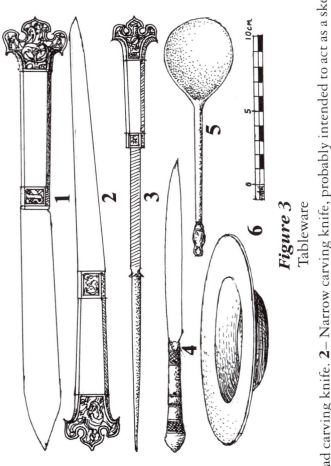

Figure 3
Tableware

1– Broad carving knife. **2–** Narrow carving knife, probably intended to act as a skewer to hold venison in place while carving it with the broad knife. **3–** Steel to sharpen the carving knives. **4–** Eating knife. **5–** Silver spoon. **6–** Silver saucer for sauces such as mustard etc.

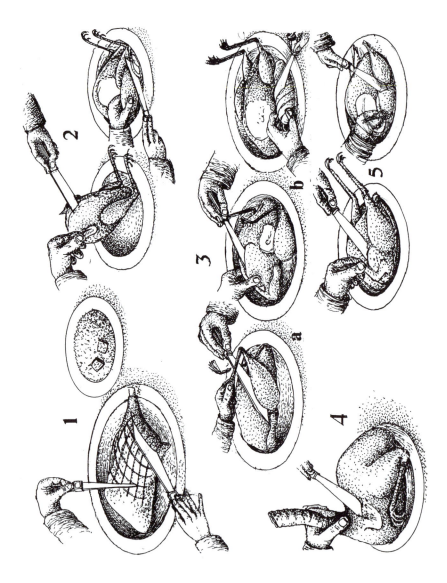

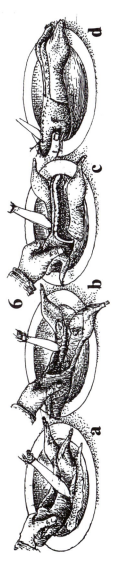

Figure 4

Carving

1– Holding venison firm with one knife, the other is used to cut in squares and lay it on a bed of frumenty. **2**– Pheasants, chickens etc. had their wings cut off and finely chopped in syrup. **3**– Goose etc., the legs removed first (a), then the wings (b), these being arranged as shown (c) before carving. **4**– Peacock had the wing cut off and carved, but the lower legs were kept intact. **5**– Capons, hens etc. had their wings removed, then their thighs, these being chopped finely and sprinkled with ale or wine. **6**– Rabbits had their skin removed (a), cuts made down both sides of the lower spine (b), were turned over and their sides cut free (c), then re-assembled, the nape of the neck removed, and a side served to the lord (d).

81

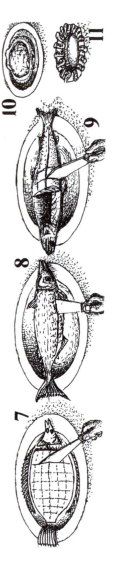

Figure 4 continued

7– Plaice had skin and fins removed before being cut into squares. **8**– Cod etc. were split down the back and had their skin, bones and roes removed. **9**– Salmon were treated similarly but were then cut into morsels for the lord's trencher. **10**– Crab meat was prepared and returned to its shell. **11**– Shrimps were peeled and set round the rim of a saucer of vinegar.

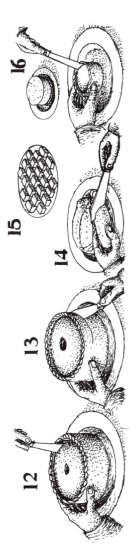

Figure 4 continued

12– Hot pies had their lids removed. **13–** Cold pies had had their lids and the upper halves of their walls cut off. **14–** Chickens lifted from the pies had their wings finely sliced and mixed with the pie juices. **15–** Custards were cut into squares. **16–** Doucettes or small flans had their walls removed before being served.

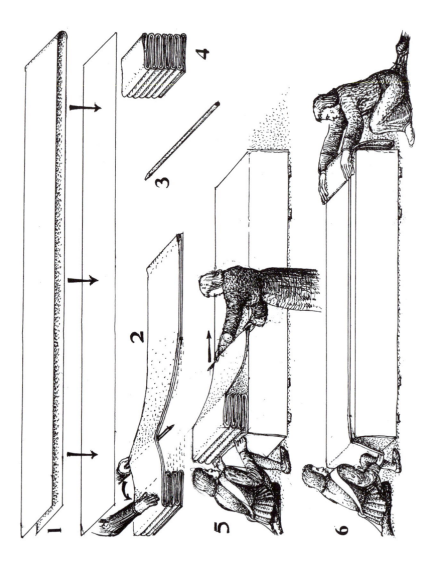

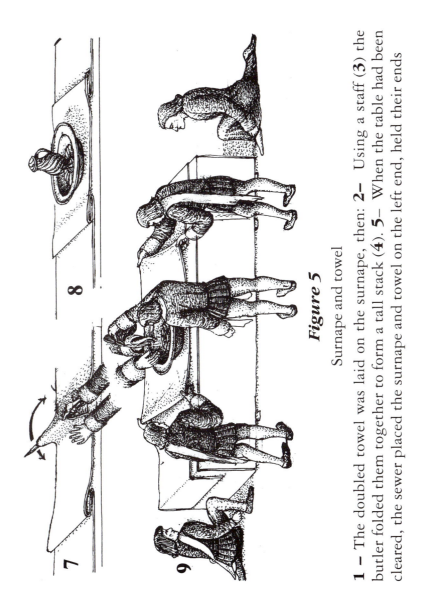

Figure 5

Surnape and towel

1 – The doubled towel was laid on the surnape, then: **2–** Using a staff (**3**) the butler folded them together to form a tall stack (**4**). **5–** When the table had been cleared, the sewer placed the surnape and towel on the left end, held their ends

continued from previous page 85

out so that the marshal could thread his staff through the towel and, gripping the surnape too, draw them both down the table. **6–** Both kneeling, the sewer and marshal pulled the cloths tight, the marshal folding the surplus up at his end. **7–** The marshal laid a nine-inch estate to each side of the lord. **8–** The ewer and basin were placed before the lord while grace was said. **9–** Two senior table-servants held up the estates beneath the lord's wrists as he washed his hands. The sewer and marshal pulled the cloths tight again, carried their ends to the centre of the table, and folded them so that the sewer could return them to the ewery table.

Figure 6

To dress a lord

1– On cold mornings the chamberlain warms the lord's breech (linen underpants) and shirt before the fire, having set a chair close by with cushions on the seat and for the feet, all covered by a sheet, ready for his master's use. Once in his breech, shirt and a short petticoat (**2**), he donned his doublet, and had the front tied together with short laces called points

(continued on next page

86

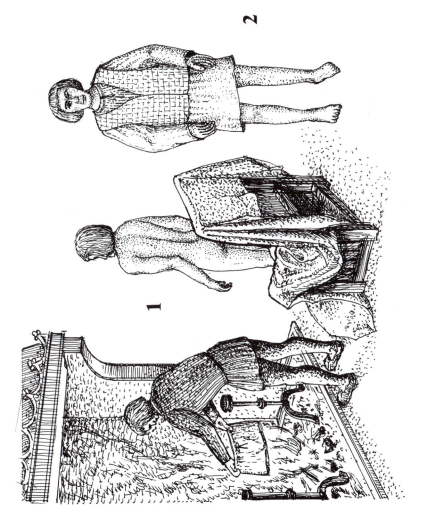

continued from previous page

(**3**) before the stomacher of rich material or elaborate slashing was secured in place (**4**). The lord's vamps (inner ankle socks) and outer socks were then put on (**5**), followed by the feet of his long hose made of woollen cloth, and his shoes (**6**). After his shirt tails had been tucked between his thighs, the hose were struck up, their waistband being trussed by points through pairs of holes around the base of the doublet (**7**). The chamberlain then wrapped a kerchief round the lord's shoulders and combed his hair (**8**), washed his hands and face, and, kneeling, asked which gown was to be worn. Now in his gown and hat, the lord was given a final brush down before setting off to church (**9**).

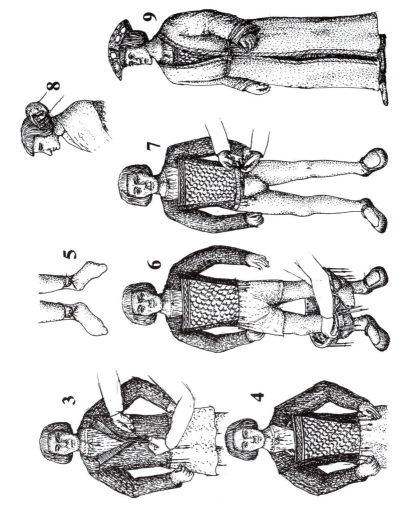

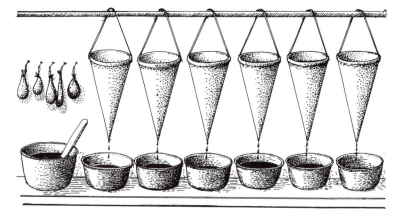

Figure 7

Hippocras

Red wine was mixed in the first bowl with spices from the bladders and a quantity of sugar. Having passed through the first two filter bags it was tasted and further spices or sugar added to balance its taste before it went on to filter through the next four bags.

Figure 8

Butler

In the buttery this butler, carved on a misericord in Ludlow parish church, fills a pot of wine by drawing the bung (seen in his left hand) from the "cannelle of box", or bung tap driven into the end of the barrel.

Figure 9

In this woodcut, printed by William Caxton some
time before 1501, we see a traveller with his satchel
(Odysseus?) at the door of a dining chamber. The

Figure 9 continued

tablecloth has two estates folded down its front, and has been set with a globular salt to the lord's right, square trenchers and round manchet loaves. At the far end of the table the butler wearing his towel round his neck fills a cup, while in the foreground a waiter wears his towel over his left shoulder.

―――――――――

GLOSSARY

GLOSSARY

Most of the unfamiliar words in the original text are explained here. For particular dishes additional references are given in the form of a Latin number followed by one in Arabic numerals. These are the 'chapter' and recipe numbers for appropriate medieval recipes printed in C.B. Hieatt & S. Butler's *Curye on Inglysh*, (Oxford 1983).

Addes, adze The cooper's adze was an axe with the blade set at right-angles to the handle on one side, and a hammer-head to the other.

Alaye The carving term for a pheasant, from *allay* in the sense of subsiding or putting down.

Ambre gelly Either an amber-coloured jelly, or one flavoured and scented with ambergris, or as in Harleian MS 4016:

Put in good quantite of saffron (that hit have faire ambur colour).

Barbe The carving term for a lobster, from *barb*, to clip or trim.

Base Bass, the common perch, *Perca fluviatilis*.

Bastarde A sweet Spanish wine similar to muscadel.

Blanket, donne or cotton These were the predecessors of toilet paper. Blanket was undyed loosely-woven woollen cloth, cotton was either smooth cloth woven from the fine fibres enclosing the seeds of the cotton plant, or a coarse woollen cloth with a raised nap which was made both in Wales and North-Western England. There are no contemporary references to any textile called donne or down. We must assume that the down of poultry or thistle was used as kingly toilet paper.

Blaunche manger 'White food.' Cooked capon or chicken ground and mixed with rice and almond milk to a paté-like consistency. There were various spicings, and almonds were often used for garnishing. II 14, 33; III 27 & IV 38, 200

Blaunche poudre Ginger ground with sugar.

Bought The central crease or fold in a tablecloth.

Brandrels, **Braundrells** White apples; the *OED* says these are now called 'calville blanc'.

Brawne The boned shoulder of wild or tame boar, cooked in wine, salt and spices, in which liquor it was kept until required. When related to poultry etc., brawne simply means their flesh.

Breche Breeches or underpants made from a wide cylinder of linen joined between the legs and having a draw-string around the top.

Brewe Probably a variety of snipe.

Browes Either small pieces of meat stewed with herbs and spices before being thickened with rice flour, bread or eggs, or else a rich meat stock poured over cubed bread.

Broche A spit, 'in broche' meaning spit-roasted.

Brytte, Brit young herring or sprats resembling whitebait.

Campolet A white wine.

Canelles of box Bung-taps made of boxwood, used for tapping barrels.

Canell Cinnamon, but probably used here for the similar but inferior cassia bark.

Capryke Probably a sweet wine from the island of Capri, or Cyprus.

Carawey in comfetes Caraway seeds given a smooth, hard sugar coating.

Cevy Civy, here a gravy in which oysters were cooked.

Chafing dish see chaufynge

Charlet A kind of custard made with milk, eggs, ground pork, saffron and salt. II 20, IV 41

Chaufynge dysshe of coles A small portable fire-basket filled with glowing charcoal. Three knobs projecting from its rim supported a dish or pan in which food could be warmed, reheated or lightly cooked at table.

Chawdron Here the usual accompaniment for roast swan, being a rich stock made from its giblets, thickened with bread and its blood and flavoured with ginger, cloves, pepper, salt and wine. IV 147

Chevene The chub, *Cyprenus* or *Leuciscus cephalus.*

Chewettes Individual baked or deep-fried pies, their pinched crusts making them resemble small cabbages or *choux.*

Chyme The ends of the staves which project beyond the flat ends of barrels.

Chychynge yron Either the cooper's driver, a short iron-headed tool used to drive down the hoops, or a flagging iron used to drive rushes or scraps of linen between the staves.

Chynne, chyne The backbone.

Chyppere The knife used to trim or chip the crusts from loaves of bread.

Claret wyne A clear yellowish or light red wine from France.

Clarrey A sweet liquor made from wine, clarified honey and spices such as ginger, pepper, cinnamon etc. IV 205 & V 6

Coffyn The pastry shell of a pie, pasty or flan.

Compost A sweet chutney-like mixture of root vegetables and fruits in vinegar, honey, salt and spices. IV 103

Cony, coney A rabbit.

Couche A tablecloth, particularly the first one that is laid on the table as a base for the upper tablecloths.

Creves In the 15th and 16th centuries the term crayfish referred to lobsters, crabs and crayfish, sea crayfish being lobsters and river crayfish, the *Astacus fluviatilis* which we recognise as crayfish today.

Culpon The carving term for a trout, from the verb culpon, meaning to cut in pieces, or slice up.

Curtesy A bow made to a superior, or to the place where he shall sit.

Custarde An open pie or flan in which either herbs or cooked meat or fish were baked in an egg-rich batter until it solidified and crusted over, hence the earlier term 'crustade'.

Doublet A close-fitting coat, with or without sleeves, usually with fastenings down the breast and pairs of holes around the waist by which it was trussed with points (laces) to the hose.

Doucettes, dowcettes Individual sweet flans filled with mixtures of eggs, honey, pork etc.

Dyaper Linen woven with an overall twill design of small diamonds.

Dyght To set in order, or array.

Egryt The lesser white heron.

Enbrewe, **imbrue** To dirty or soil.

Endoured Glazed with egg yolks or saffron and almond milk.

Estat, estate A pleat folded across a tablecloth or towel once it had been laid on the table.

Fastynge Times of fasting, as on the various feasts of the medieval church. Possibly also the early part of the day, before dinner.

Faucettes Either the peg or spile-pin used to stop the vent-hole of a barrel, or a wooden spiggot or tap by which the contents of barrels were drawn off.

Fygges of Malyke Figs from Malaga on the Mediterranean coast of Spain.

Flawnes Flans.

Fourmentye Boiled hulled wheat cooked with light stock, saffron, egg yolks etc. II 1 & IV 1

Fruche The carving term for chickens, from frush, to bruise, break or crush.

Frumenty see fourmentye

Fruyter vaunte A fritter perhaps containing a fruit mixture. A recipe for a vaunt is printed in the 1594 *Good Huswifes Handmaid for the Kitchen.*

Fruyter saye, fruyter sayge Perhaps a sage-rich version of frytour of erbes. IV 156

Fruyter pouche Presumably a fritter formed as a pocket or pouch of pastry with a rich filling, rather than the alternative of a fritter based on a fish stomach, or a variation of pochee (IV 92), a dish of poached eggs in a thick sauce of milk and egg yolks.

Fumosytees, fumosities Those parts of foods which caused indigestion, their fumes rising from the stomach to the brain, and thus inducing headaches.

Fyne The carving term for the chub, meaning to remove the fins.

Galentyne Either the jelly (Latin *galatina*) produced when cooking fish, such as the set juices in lamprey pies, or a sauce made by thickening this with breadcrumbs and spices. I 51 & III 24. Also a spiced sauce thickened with breadcrumbs and usually containing galingale. IV 131

Gamelyne Sauce camelyne (IV 49) made with ground currants, walnuts, bread, spices, including cinnamon (canell) mixed with vinegar.

Gelopere Furnival (p.173) suggests that this sauce was made with clove gillyflowers (pinks), but it is much more likely to be sauce alepeuer or olypeuer (Harleian MS 4016 & Ashmole MS 1439) made by soaking toast in vinegar and mixing it with salt and pepper.

Gobone, Gobbon To cut in pieces, or a piece, slice or gobbet (mouth-sized portion) so cut.

Graynes of paradico, grains of paradise The hot-flavoured capsules of *Amomum Meleguetta.*

Grene fysshe, green fish Fresh or unsalted fish, especially the cod and codling.

Heedshete A sheet at the head of a bed, probably laid over the pillow. Henry VIII had one made of cambric (*Inventory* 12686).

Hen of grece A fat hen.

Herynge, whyte Fresh herring.

Hippocras see ipocras

Hony, Heere Hair. (Furnival p.140)

Hose A garment made of woollen cloth which extended from the toes up to the waist, where it was pierced by pairs of holes for points (laces) by which it was trussed to the bottom edge of the doublet.

Hot, cold, dry and moist The four humours were based on the idea that four major fluids made up the human body, originating with the theories of Hippocrates, fourth century BC.

Houndefysshe A small shark, such as the didfish.

Householde brede Bread made from wholewheat flour from which the fine white flour had been extracted by boulting. This bread was usually raised by a sourdough yeast.

Hurtelberyes Whortleberries or bilberries, *Vaccinium Myrtillus.*

Ipocras Red wine (but also white in other texts) in which spices were soaked and sugar dissolved, after which it was filtered to make a digestive liquor to be served at the end of a meal. A recipe in Furnival (pp. 362–3) gives the proportions of the spices as 10 parts cinnamon, 4 parts ginger, 1 part grains of paradise and four parts sugar.

Joll The head and 'shoulders' of large fishes such as sturgeon and salmon.

Jouncat A cream cheese made in a rush basket or strained and served on a rush mat.

Jowtes A selection of herbs boiled, chopped small and cooked either in a rich broth or almond milk, sugar and salt.

Jussel A boiled mixture of eggs and broth, usually thickened with breadcrumbs and flavoured with saffron, sage and salt.

Leach see leche

Leche and lombarde Made up of ground pork, eggs, dried fruit, salt, sugar and spices cooked in a bladder, sliced, and served in a spiced wine and almond milk sauce. IV 66

Leche dewgarde A variety of slice, but no recipe with this title appears to have been located to date.

Leche, whyte Probably a milk, sugar and rosewater jelly cut into slices. A later version was published in Thomas Dawson's *Good Huswifes Jewell* of 1596.

Lesche To slice. The carving term for brawn.

Lofe In this text, the loaf appears to refer to the manchet, a round yeast-raised white wheaten roll, set around the perimeter and pricked in the centre before baking.

Longe peper This spice comes from two species of the pepper plant, *Piper longum* coming from the foot of the Himalayas and southern India, and *Piper retrofractum*, the more pungent, from Malaysia.

Lyes Lees, the sediment deposited in the bottoms of barrels of wine.

Malvesy Malmsey, a strong sweet wine from the neighbourhood of Monemvasia at the southern tip of Morea in southern Greece.

Mamony, marmony A dish usually made of minced poultry cooked with spiced wine and/or almond milk. I 7; II 30; III 25 & IV 22, 202

Martynet The house-martin, a bird of the swallow family, *Chalidon urbica*.

Mawe The stomach.

Menewes Minnows.

Messe When diners sat at both sides of long tables, they were notionally divided into messes of four people, two set to each side. Each of these messes then received a mess (a serving for four people) of each dish on the menu, e.g. a mess of potage. The 'second mess' was that served to the individual or small group seated to the lord's left on the top table.

Morter Either a bowl of wax with a floating wick, or a short thick candle, used as a nightlight in bedrooms etc.

Mortrus See potage.

Muscadell A strong sweet wine made from the muscat grape.

Musculade A mussel sauce?

Mynce To chop in very small pieces using the carving knife.

Nombles of a dere Umbles, the edible innards or pluck of a deer, used to make umble pie.

Osey A sweet French wine, *vin d'Aussai*, from Alsace.

Panter The officer in charge of the bread both in the pantry and during its service at table. This office was sometimes combined with that of butler.

Payn Puffe A rich filling enclosed in a round 'loaf' made from flour, cream, egg yolks and sugar. IV 204

Pegyll The *Liber Cure Cocorum* (quoted by Furnival p.74) states that to make this sauce one should

> Take dropping of capon rosted well,
> With wyne and mustarde as thou eele (bliss),
> With onyons smalle schrad and sothun in grece,
> Meng alle fere and forthe hit messe.

Harleian MS 4016 provides a recipe for pykkyll for mallard which has fried onions, beef broth, white pepper, cinnamon, mustard, ginger and mallard dripping.

Peson, pessene Peas, usually a potage of dried peas unless fresh peas were in season.

Pestelles The back legs, invariably those of pigs.

Pety peruant A mixture of ox bone marrow, egg yolks, minced dates, currants, salt, sugar and ginger, made into small round pasties or pies in a flour, egg yolk, saffron and salt crust, then baked or deep-fried.

Pety peruys Furnival (p.32 note 3 & p.157) suggests that these were identical to the above, and that the 'u' is in error for an 'n'. In the absence of any other evidence, this appears to be the most probable explanation.

Plyte To fold or pleat, or the pleat so formed.

Portenaunce The innards or pluck of an animal, particularly those of lambs.

Posset A thick spoonable drink of hot milk and, perhaps, eggs set by the action of ale, wine etc.

Potell The measure of half a gallon, or four pints.

Potage In its simplest form, the stock from boiled meat enriched with vegetables, oatmeal etc., but also one of the thick foods such as frumenty, worts, marmony, mortrus etc. used to accompany meats and fish.

Powled Its meaning is uncertain, but its context suggests that it indicated staleness or a sour fermentation in ale.

Standarde The principal or standing dish to be set on a table.

Stocke fysshe Air-dried cod, haddock, hake, ling etc.

Subtylte, subtlety An ornamental dish usually made of sugar, marchpane (marzipan) or wax, which depicted some three-dimensional device such as a group of saints, a model building or ship etc., frequently bearing scrolls inscribed with appropriate mottoes.

Surnape A long narrow tablecloth laid over the main tablecloths and beneath the towel just before hand-washing.

Syde The carving term for a pig or a haddock, probably from 'side', meaning to put aside or tidy away.

Syrupe Almonds ground in wine, then stewed with pine nuts, currants, saffron, cloves, cinnamon and sugar, which was poured over capons, hens, chickens, stockdove and salmon prior to carving.

Tansey An omelet flavoured with the juice of tansy (*Tanacetum vulgare*), an extremely bitter herb.

Tarryour An augur used for boring tapering bung-holes in barrels.

Thorpole, threpole A thirlepoll or whale.

Tornsole A violet-blue or purple food colouring obtained from the plant *Crozophora Tinctoria*, usually supplied in the form of pieces of linen impregnated with its juice.

Towell of Reynes A towel of fine linen made at Rennes in Brittany.

Trassene The carving term for an eel, from transon, to cut into segments or pieces.

Traunche The carving term for a sturgeon. Also, to slice, or a slice of anything.

Trenchours Square slices of four-day-old sourdough wheaten bread, from which the fine white flour had been extracted. They were used by diners as personal cutting-boards.

Trumpe The passage of the crane's windpipe between two plates of bone which lined the keel of its sternum. The carver was advised to avoid this feature.

Turnsole See tornsole

Turrentyne, torrentyne Both Russell (Furnival pp. 38 & 57) and the *Boke* list this fish along with salt porpoise, seal and sturgeon, suggesting that it was a large marine creature. A quotation in Furnival (p.107) states that a fish *Magnus thunnus* from the Gulf of Taranto (between the 'heel' and 'toe' of Italy), was known as the tarentella or tarentino in Italy. It would therefore appear most probable that torrentyne was imported salt tuna, *Thunnus thynaus*. The alternative, a trout, is unlikely, since there are quite separate references to trout in both Russell and the *Boke*.

Tuske The carving term for a barbel, perhaps referring to the fleshy tusk-like protuberances dangling from its upper jaw.

Tyere The carving term for an egg. Andrew Boorde's *Dyetary of Helth* of 1542 says that eggs are 'tyred with a lytell salte and suger'.

Tyerre A sweet wine either from Tyre in Syria, or probably a Calabrian or Sicilian wine made from the tirio species of grape.

Unlace The carving term for a coney or rabbit.

Urynall The common 16th-century urinal took the form of a flat-bottomed globular earthenware vessel with a looped handle mounted above a round hole on top. For a lord, it may also have been a glass vessel with which his physician could examine the state of his water.

Vergyus, verjuice The acid juice of the green or unripe grape, often replaced in England by the raw juice of crab-apples.

Vernage A strong, sweet Italian wine.

Vernage wyne cut Cut, or cuit, was new wine reduced by boiling and given added sweetening. It was used both as a drink, and as an addition to weaker wines in order to improve their keeping qualities.

Voyde To clear the table. Also the small final course of wafers, hippocras and sweetmeats served at this stage of the meal.

Ware A misprint for wax, a wax candle to be set in the lord's bedchamber.

Wortes Vegetables such as cabbages, beets, leeks, nettles and various other herbs, parboiled, chopped small with oatmeal, and cooked in stock.

Wrapper The purpayne. See above.

Wynges In carving poultry and gamebirds, the wing was the wing itself and a large area of the surrounding breast. The shoulders of rabbits and hares were also known as wings.

APPENDIX

APPENDIX

Accompaniments, Syrup, Sprinklings and Sauces

The following table has been compiled from *The Boke of Keruynge* and John Russell's *Boke of Nurture* to provide a direct means of determining the carving terms and recommended accompaniments etc. for each particular item of food.

The Accompaniments

Potages (1)
Frumenty
Pease
Wortes
Syrup

Sprinklings after carving (2)
Ale
Cinnamon
Ginger
Salt
Salt & cinnamon
Sugar
Sugar, salt & water
Verjuice
Vinegar
Vinegar & ginger
Vinegar, cinnamon & ginger

Wine
Wine, vinegar & salt

Sauces (3)
Butter
Chawdron
Galantine
Gamelyne sauce
Garlic, vinegar or pepper
Ginger sauce
Ginger or mustard with
  verjuice & pepper
Ginger, cinnamon & red wine
Ginger, mustard, vinegar & salt
Green sauce
Mustard
Mustard & sugar
Onions, boiled
Pike sauce

Meat	*Carving Term*	**Accompaniment**
Bacon		pease (1)
Beef		wortes (1); mustard (3)
Beef, roast		garlic, vinegar or pepper (3)
Brawn	*Lesche*	mustard (3)
Coney	*Unlace*	wortes (1);
		vinegar & ginger (2);
		mustard & sugar (3)
Fawn		ginger sauce (3)
Hare		wortes (1)
Kid		sugar (2)
Lamb		gamelyne sauce (3)
Mutton		mustard (3)
Pig		ginger sauce (3)
Veal		verjuice (2)
Venison	*Break*	salt & cinnamon (2)

Poultry etc.

Bittern	*Unjoint*	salt (2); gamelyne sauce (3)
Bustard		gamelyne sauce (3)
Capon	*Sauce*	syrup (1); verjuice (2);
		green sauce (3)
Chicken		syrup (1); verjuice (2);
		green sauce (3)

Crane .... *Display* .... verjuice (2); ginger, mustard,
vinegar & salt (3)

Curlew .... *Untache* .... salt (2);
sugar, salt & water (2)

Egret .... salt (2)

Goose .... *Rear* .... no accompaniment

Hen .... *Spoil* .... syrup (1); verjuice (2);
green sauce (3)

Heron .... *Dismember* .... ginger, mustard, vinegar
& salt (3)

Lapwing, Lark
& Martin .... salt & cinnamon (2)

Mallard .... *Unbrace* .... no accompaniment

Partridge .... *Wing* .... wine, vinegar & salt (2)
mustard & sugar (3)

Peacock .... *Disfigure* .... no accompaniment

Pheasant .... *Allay* .... mustard & sugar (3)

Pigeon .... *Thigh* .... no accompaniment

Plover .... *Mince* .... salt (2); gamelyne sauce (3)

Quail .... *Wing* .... salt (2); salt & cinnamon(2)

Stockdove .... syrup (1)

Shoveller .... ginger (2)

Snipe .... salt (2)

Sparrow .... *Thigh* .... salt (2)

Swan .... chawdron (3)

Thrush............ *Thigh* .... salt & cinnamon (2)

Woodcock........ *Thigh* .... salt & cinnamon (2)

Fish

Barbel............ *Tusk*............ no accompaniment

Beaver tail....................... frumenty (1); pease (1)

Bream............ *Splay* .... vinegar, cinnamon
& ginger (2)

Carp........................... cinnamon (2)

Chub .... *Fin* .... cinnamon (2)

Cod........................ ginger or mustard with
verjuice & pepper (3)

Cod, salt .... mustard (3)

Conger eel..................... mustard (3)

Crab .... *Tame* .... vinegar (2); vinegar,
cinnamon & ginger (2)

Crayfish .... vinegar, cinnamon
& ginger (2)

Dace .... verjuice (2)

Eel .... *Trassene* .... vinegar, cinnamon
& ginger (2)

Eel, salt .... mustard (3)

Flounder .... cinnamon (2)

Gurnard..................... vinegar, cinnamon
& ginger (3)

Gurnard, salt..................... mustard (3)

Haddock........... *Side* .... ginger or mustard with
  verjuice & pepper (3)

Hake................................ ginger or mustard with
  verjuice & pepper (3)

Herring .... salt (2)

Herring, baked .... sugar (2)

Herring, salt .... mustard (3)

Houndfish .... ginger or mustard with
  verjuice & pepper (3)

Lamprey .... *String* .... vinegar, cinnamon
  & ginger (2); ginger,
  cinnamon & red wine (3)

Ling.................................. green sauce (3)

Ling, salt............................. mustard (3)

Lobster .... *Barb* .... no accompaniment

Mackerel............................. butter (3)

Mackerel, salt......................... mustard (3)

Mullet .... verjuice (2); vinegar (2)

Perch .... vinegar, cinnamon &
  ginger (2); ginger or
  mustard with verjuice &
  pepper (3)

Pike .... *Splat* .... pike sauce (3)

Plaice .... *Sauce* .... wine (2); salt (2) & wine (2)

Porpoise........... *Undertranche*.... vinegar, cinnamon
  & ginger (2)

118

Porpoise, salt		frumenty (1); pease (1); vinegar (2)
Roach		verjuice (2); vinegar, cinnamon & ginger (2)
Salmon	*Chine*	syrup (1)
Salmon, salt		mustard (3)
Seal, salt		frumenty (1)
Shrimps		vinegar (2)
Sole		verjuice (2); vinegar (2)
Sturgeon, salt...*Tranche*		vinegar (2)
Swordfish, salt		vinegar (2); wine (2)
Tench	*Sauce*	no accompaniment
Thornback		ginger or mustard with verjuice & pepper (3)
Thornback, salt		ginger (2)
Trout, salt	*Culpon*	vinegar (2)
Turbot		green sauce (3)
Whale, salt		vinegar, cinnamon & ginger (2)
Whiting		butter (3)

Miscellaneous

Egg	*Tyre*	no accompaniment
Pasty	*Border*	no accompaniment

Wynkyn de Worde (Jan van Wynkyn)

born at Wörth, Alsace; died in London, *c* 1535

*T*HE BOKE OF KERUYNGE was published in 1508 and printed by Wynkyn de Worde, Caxton's distinguished successor. When Caxton returned to England in 1476 after thirty years abroad he set up at the Sign of the Red Pale in the precincts of Westminster Abbey, bringing Wynkyn de Worde with him as foreman of his printing house.

Caxton had been in Cologne and Bruges, where the new art of printing with moveable types was being practised, and brought much of his equipment from the Continent, including some fonts. On Caxton's death in 1491 de Worde inherited all his presses and typefaces, and continued to use these for another ten years.

In those years he printed a hundred titles, including a new edition of Caxton's *The Golden Legend* (a popular ecclesiastical anthology) in 1493, and, in 1496, of his *Boke of St Alban's*, a sporting handbook with added material on fishing.

He was soon joined by three other printers: the Frenchman Barbier (probably at his invitation), Julian Notary, and another whose name has not survived, and the firm's total output, including broadsheets and new editions, eventually reached 800 titles.

Wynkyn de Worde seems to have cut his own types. This is a very specialised skill. Lead, tin and pewter were some of the metals used at that time for the typefaces, which were hardened with antimony, iron or bismuth; steel and brass were among the materials that made up the moulds. After 1500 he began to recut some of the fonts he had inherited, achieving a great degree of perfection with Caxton's Black Letter – the font in which *The Book of Keruynge* is set. The letters are beautifully clean, clear and readable and the spacing and design of the page very satisfying.

Wynkyn de Worde lived in Fleet Street, London.

———————————

De Ricci's *A Census of Caxtons* (Bibliographical Society's Monograph No XV, 1909) gives a list of typefaces used by Caxton and another of books printed by Wynkyn de Worde after Caxton's death.

———————————